Milady's Master Educator
Exam Review

for Trainees to Become Educators
in the Fields of Cosmetology, Barber Styling,
Massage, Nail Technology, and Esthetics

Letha Barnes

Printed in Canada
6 7 8 9 10 XXX 06

For more information contact Milady,
3 Columbia Circle, PO Box 15015
Albany, NY 12212-5015

Or find us on the World Wide Web at http://www.Milady.com

ISBN: 1-56253-733-4
Library of Congress Catalog Card Number: 00-032431

Contents

1 History of Teaching

1. To "educate" has been defined as training by formal instruction and supervised ________ especially in a skill, trade, or profession.
   a. skills c. ability
   b. practice d. observation ______

2. To "educate" has been defined as developing mentally, morally, or aesthetically, especially by ________.
   a. demonstration c. instruction
   b. lecturing d. role-playing ______

3. The primary focus of the educator is to ________ education and training in the appropriate practical discipline.
   a. enforce c. dictate
   b. provide d. administer ______

4. The primary purpose of cosmetology schools and those in related disciplines is to train competent, qualified professionals for successful ________ in their chosen field.
   a. downtime c. employment
   b. retirement d. attitudes ______

5. Available positions for the cosmetology educator are Phase I Instructor, Theory Instructor, Director of Student Affairs, or:
   a. Director of Admissions c. Director of Education
   b. Director of Financial Aid d. President ______

6. A cosmetology educator must have a passion for the beauty and image industry and at the same time have ________ for the students.
   a. pessimism c. nonchalance
   b. discipline d. compassion ______

7. The educational arm of the American Association of Cosmetology Schools (AACS) is the:
   a. Department of Education
   b. Cosmetology Educators of America
   c. Teachers Educational Council
   d. Cosmetology Teachers Association _____

8. The philosopher who believed that an educator should be concerned first with the physical and mental development of their students and then to the subject matter being taught was:
   a. Johann Friedrich Herbart
   b. Ronald Reagan
   c. Jean-Jacques Rousseau
   d. John Dewey _____

9. The report *A Nation at Risk* acknowledged that teaching as a profession had become increasingly demanding in the United States due to:
   a. diverse student populations
   b. inaccessible education
   c. cost of education
   d. students' unwillingness to learn _____

10. Instruction in skills necessary for persons who are preparing to enter the workforce or who need training or retraining in the technology of their occupation is known as:
    a. secondary education
    b. college education
    c. primary education
    d. vocational education _____

11. The master educator of the future must stay ________ of the changes in conditions affecting student groups in the classroom.
    a. ignorant
    b. abreast
    c. unaware
    d. unmindful _____

12. In the early 1980s, teaching by ________ was considered an acceptable method of teaching, but is now considered obsolete.
    a. discipline
    b. example
    c. threat
    d. observation _____

13. Dynamic educators convey the spirit and love of learning to their students and stress the value of ________ and ________ above ignorance.
    a. learning and knowledge
    b. learning and socializing
    c. socializing and knowledge
    d. insensibility and socializing _____

14. To succeed as a master educator, you need to create the correct mix of self-motivation, ________, technical skills, effective communication, and a strong work ethic.
    a. sincerity
    b. indifference
    c. authority
    d. complacency _____

15. For a career field to be considered a profession, it must provide both ________ and social services that are essential.
    a. physical
    b. personal
    c. spiritual
    d. metaphysical _____

16. To be considered a profession, the career field must command a body of ________ and involves intellectual activities.
    a. technical skills
    b. theoretical ability
    c. specialized knowledge
    d. practical ability _____

17. One criterion for a career field to be considered a/an ________ is that it relies on theory that has been drawn from basic foundational skills that can be applied to its practice.
    a. job
    b. profession
    c. avocation
    d. hobby _____

18. The members of a profession enjoy a wide range of ________ and freedom in making decisions and professional judgments.
    a. autonomy
    b. dependence
    c. civil liberties
    d. perquisites _____

19. Higher educational requirements for employment, changing technology, and the need for specialized training have made ________ preparation imperative.
    a. elementary
    b. occupational
    c. attitudinal
    d. emotional _____

20. The master educator of the future will focus on participant-centered, ________ education to ensure that all students understand and retain the material presented.
    a. theory-oriented
    b. computer-oriented
    c. discovery-oriented
    d. teacher-centered _____

2 The Profile of a Master Educator

1. The basic function of the educator is to:
   a. facilitate learning
   b. provide entertainment
   c. be a social director
   d. be a counselor _____

2. Teaching is an intellectual experience that demands the ability to invent and ________ new techniques and procedures to meet the changing demands of learners and the industry.
   a. reject
   b. copy
   c. adapt
   d. misapply _____

3. One of the most frequently cited characteristics that school owners require in their educators is:
   a. discipline
   b. loyalty
   c. humor
   d. friendship _____

4. Educators must remain open to the knowledge of:
   a. their own experience
   b. only the textbook
   c. only the lesson plans
   d. all those around them _____

5. Education is a continuing process; changes and improvements in techniques and technology within cosmetology and related fields occur:
   a. daily
   b. weekly
   c. monthly
   d. yearly _____

6. A good rule of thumb for effective professional development as an educator is to obtain how many hours of continuing education per year?
   a. 12
   b. 20
   c. 30
   d. 40 _____

7. ________ is one of the most valuable resources of life, and every human being has exactly the same amount of it.
   a. Education c. Time
   b. Knowledge d. Money _____

8. What will determine the general direction of your life and energy?
   a. circumstances c. luck
   b. goals d. determination _____

9. Managing time effectively is mastering ________.
   a. life's nuances c. event control
   b. basic elements d. theoretical skills _____

10. Putting off until tomorrow what can be accomplished today is known as:
    a. indifference c. forgetfulness
    b. procrastination d. laziness _____

11. When an individual is cited or appealed to as an expert and thus has the power to influence or command thought, opinion, or behavior, he is considered to be a/an:
    a. authority c. professional
    b. know-it-all d. diplomat _____

12. Steps to build self-confidence are liking and accepting yourself, practicing self-control, becoming good at what you do, and being:
    a. critical of others c. helpful to others
    b. true to yourself d. true to friends _____

13. Having authority in the classroom requires that the master educator establish a ________ between themselves and their learners.
    a. close friendship c. close proximity
    b. close relationship d. formal distance _____

14. Educators who are of high moral ________ and firmness and who hold a set of moral principles or values that are above reproach are in great demand in the workforce.
    a. goals c. excellence
    b. purpose d. relationships _____

15. In the school, a dynamic team will share a spirit of passion and focus on:
    a. individual goals
    b. the same goals
    c. personal beliefs
    d. inconsistent goals ____

16. To understand and know what is expected of you in your educator role within an institution, refer to the:
    a. student handbook
    b. position description
    c. state laws
    d. rules and regulations ____

17. When your ________ rises, you will be able to take action without worrying that the action is the right thing to do.
    a. paycheck
    b. attitude
    c. self-confidence
    d. ego ____

18. To turn challenges into opportunities with ease, the educator must be sincere, patient, and in:
    a. control
    b. competition
    c. love
    d. harmony ____

19. Qualities essential to success as a master educator are courtesy, compassion, and:
    a. inconsistency
    b. consistency
    c. intolerance
    d. culture ____

20. The ingredient that makes the difference between an average educator and a master educator is:
    a. luck
    b. education
    c. opportunity
    d. desire ____

21. The driving force behind everything an individual will accomplish, whether positive or negative, intentional or unintentional, is:
    a. motivation
    b. emotion
    c. manipulation
    d. apathy ____

22. The term ________ is derived from the Greek word *enthous*, which means inspired.
    a. eagerness
    b. enterprising
    c. enthusiasm
    d. excitement ____

23. A master educator must ________ working with students.
    a. tolerate
    b. enjoy
    c. avoid
    d. endure ____

24. Any chance for happiness or success can be squelched by:
    a. enthusiasm
    b. optimism
    c. tolerance
    d. negativism _____

25. Effective ________ skills are needed to reach a variety of generations and backgrounds in today's learners.
    a. communication
    b. technical
    c. vocational
    d. theoretical _____

3 Educator Relationships

1. The state of affairs existing between those who have an aspect or quality that ________ them as being or working together is referred to as a relationship.
   a. detaches c. employs
   b. connects d. forces ____

2. An essential element of communicating is:
   a. listening c. discussing
   b. talking d. interrupting ____

3. An educator who wants a good educator–learner relationship seeks ________ to make adjustments in teaching techniques and to meet the needs of individual learners.
   a. praise c. feedback
   b. compliments d. evaluation ____

4. The master educator will be genuinely interested in all learners, know and pronounce correctly the name of each learner, make learners feel important, and:
   a. be stubborn c. be authoritarian
   b. be moody d. be cheerful ____

5. The master educator will take the initiative to give ________ and compliments to the learner.
   a. gifts c. praise
   b. reprimands d. complaints ____

6. The ability of educators to work together toward a common vision is known as:
   a. individuality c. indirectness
   b. teamwork d. aimless ____

7. To build strong relationships with other educators, the master educator will never ________ the work of other educators.
   a. criticize   c. approve
   b. share   d. transfer   _____

8. To ensure a positive relationship with superiors, the master educator will verify questionable information, follow instructions, provide thorough and accurate reports, and be:
   a. critical   c. authoritative
   b. intolerant   d. observant   _____

9. School personnel may not discuss an eligible student's performance with a family member without ________ consent from the eligible student.
   a. verbal   c. written
   b. expressed   d. stated   _____

10. In developing positive relationships the master educator will take a/an ________ approach.
   a. indifferent   c. leisurely
   b. proactive   d. inactive   _____

11. The ability of the staff and faculty to extend themselves to meet the needs of the public plays a large role in how the institution is ________ by its consumers.
   a. misunderstood   c. perceived
   b. misjudged   d. ignored   _____

12. When another educator shines, the master educator will:
   a. share in the joy   c. reject all the success
   b. refuse to be involved   d. share in the resentment   _____

13. Master educators will recognize that there is a point in time when the ownership of a plan or idea must be ________ another individual or group.
   a. processed for   c. carried over
   b. transferred to   d. withdrawn from   _____

14. A master educator will ________ share knowledge, thoughts, and ideas with other educators.
   a. reluctantly   c. eagerly
   b. timidly   d. unwillingly   _____

15. Students who hear educators talking negatively about a student or colleague will become ________ and fear that you may feel the same way toward them.
    a. distrustful
    b. overconfident
    c. unsure
    d. intimidated ______

4 Developing a Dynamic Program of Study

1. A properly developed program of study results in a/an ________ process in which students progress satisfactorily through the course and achieve pre-established objectives.
   a. irregular
   b. systematic
   c. arbitrary
   d. enigmatic ____

2. The first step in curriculum development is to determine:
   a. class scheduling
   b. evaluation methods
   c. content resources
   d. hour units ____

3. Information obtained in step one of the curriculum development process must be ________ and assessed as to whether additional information is needed to supplement the content.
   a. gathered
   b. compiled
   c. reviewed
   d. collated ____

4. A key element in curriculum development is to identify the essential ________ knowledge, skills, and competencies needed by professionals within the field of study.
   a. mathematical
   b. occupational
   c. practical
   d. analytical ____

5. In curriculum development, the various topics and tasks to be taught must be logically ________ into related groups.
   a. organized
   b. sequenced
   c. determined
   d. evaluated ____

6. Once the subjects or categories of study have been determined, they must be logically ________.
   a. organized
   b. sequenced
   c. determined
   d. evaluated ____

7. Another important step in the curriculum development process is to ________ for each subject or category.
   a. allot grades
   b. establish schedules
   c. allocate time
   d. analyze lessons
   _____

8. A/An ________ of instruction concentrates on only one or a few of the topics within a specific subject area.
   a. lesson
   b. hour
   c. schedule
   d. unit
   _____

9. A school must determine how many ________ will be spent in each of the various units within each subject or category.
   a. hours
   b. days
   c. weeks
   d. months
   _____

10. A written plan of instruction that includes a general course description, learning goals, resources, format, grading procedures, supplies, and facilities is called a/an:
    a. lesson plan
    b. course outline
    c. class schedule
    d. orientation program
    _____

11. The road map for each class session that ensures the students receive the detailed information needed for each unit of study is the:
    a. lesson plan
    b. course outline
    c. class schedule
    d. orientation program
    _____

12. ________ is the collection and analysis of information that leads to a judgment concerning the learner's performance.
    a. Comprehension
    b. Allocation
    c. Evaluation
    d. Transformation
    _____

13. The course ________ covers the entire course of study and coordinates with the lesson plans.
    a. outline
    b. syllabus
    c. schedule
    d. evaluation
    _____

14. That part of a course or program that covers the course outline, school policies and procedures, and any other general information pertinent to the student's success is called:
    a. orientation
    b. allocation
    c. evaluation
    d. introduction
    _____

15. A/An ________ can be useful in curriculum development by drawing on their own education, experience, and familiarity with the current needs of the industry.
    a. parent/teacher association c. faculty roundtable
    b. CEO group d. advisory council ____

16. The key elements of course development revolve around intended learner ________, which are reflected in various goals and objectives.
    a. beliefs c. expectations
    b. outcomes d. attitudes ____

17. The terms *goals*, *aims*, *objectives*, and ________ are often used interchangeably in the context of education.
    a. outcomes c. expectations
    b. targets d. destinations ____

18. When defining goals and objectives, it is helpful if the educator relates to the different types of ________ that need to be specified.
    a. performances c. attitudes
    b. theories d. emotions ____

19. When the intended learning for the student is to acquire knowledge, it is known as the ________ domain of instructional outcomes.
    a. affective c. relative
    b. psychomotor d. cognitive ____

20. When the intended learning for the student is related to the performance of a specific task or activity, it is considered:
    a. affective c. cognitive
    b. psychomotor d. relative ____

21. When the intended learning for a student reflects a desire for the development of an attitude or value, it is known as:
    a. affective c. cognitive
    b. psychomotor d. relative ____

22. There are six levels of performance within the ________ domain that move from the simple to the complex.
    a. affective c. cognitive
    b. psychomotor d. relative ____

23. Recognition and recall of facts and specifics or eliciting of factual answers is the ________ level within the cognitive domain.
    a. evaluation
    b. knowledge
    c. application
    d. analysis ____

24. The ability to use or apply information in a situation different from the original learning context is the ________ level of the cognitive domain.
    a. evaluation
    b. knowledge
    c. application
    d. analysis ____

25. Interpreting, translating, summarizing, or paraphrasing given information is the ________ level of the cognitive domain.
    a. knowledge
    b. comprehension
    c. synthesis
    d. analysis ____

26. Acting, judging, or making choices based on criteria and rationale is the ________ level within the cognitive domain.
    a. knowledge
    b. evaluation
    c. synthesis
    d. analysis ____

27. The ability to separate wholes into parts until the relationships among elements are clear is known as the ________ level within the cognitive domain.
    a. knowledge
    b. evaluation
    c. synthesis
    d. analysis ____

28. Verbs such as *create*, *make*, *choose*, *solve*, *plan*, *design*, *compose*, *formulate*, and *develop* are used to write objectives for the ________ level within the cognitive domain.
    a. knowledge
    b. evaluation
    c. synthesis
    d. analysis ____

29. Verbs such as *judge*, *appraise*, *criticize*, *defend*, and *compare* are used in writing objectives for the ________ level within the cognitive domain.
    a. knowledge
    b. evaluation
    c. synthesis
    d. analysis ____

30. Verbs such as *identify*, *describe*, *define*, *match*, *select*, *choose*, *relate*, *list*, *state*, or *tell* are used in writing objectives for the ________ level within the cognitive domain.
    a. knowledge
    b. comprehension
    c. application
    d. synthesis ____

31. Verbs such as *classify*, *infer*, *indicate*, *translate*, *explain*, or *represent* are used when writing educational objectives for the ________ level within the cognitive domain.
a. knowledge
b. comprehension
c. application
d. synthesis
_____

32. Verbs such as *predict*, *choose*, *identify*, *tell*, *select*, or *explain* are used to write educational objectives for the ________ level within the cognitive domain.
a. knowledge
b. comprehension
c. application
d. synthesis
_____

33. Verbs such as *distinguish*, *describe*, *relate* and *conclude* are used to write educational objectives for the ________ level within the cognitive domain.
a. application
b. analysis
c. synthesis
d. evaluation
_____

34. The master educator's goal is to ensure that graduates can think ________ and creatively.
a. by rote
b. quickly
c. critically
d. slowly
_____

35. Objectives in the psychomotor domain relate to skill ________, which involves the manipulation of tools, objects, supplies, and equipment.
a. evaluation
b. acquisition
c. comprehension
d. performance
_____

36. In the ________ domain the desired performance involves the demonstration of feelings, attitudes, or sensitivities toward other people, ideas, or things.
a. cognitive
b. psychomotor
c. affective
d. relative
_____

37. Employers prefer to hire educators who have positive attitudes and a good work ethic, get along well with fellow workers, and are ________ in their profession.
a. happy
b. situated
c. established
d. comfortable
_____

38. Objectives serve little purpose unless they are ________ and unless efforts are made to assess their achievement.
a. clear
b. written
c. measurable
d. followed
_____

39. The most critical component of any lesson plan, which prepares the students for the upcoming instructional tasks and the purpose of the lesson, is the:
    a. prior student assignments
    b. educator references
    c. notes to educator
    d. learning motivation ______

40. The process of getting the student ready to learn is the:
    a. preparatory set
    b. anticipatory set
    c. orientation program
    d. verbal presentation ______

41. How often should the educator vary the stimuli for the students?
    a. every 5 minutes
    b. every 8 minutes
    c. every 15 minutes
    d. every 30 minutes ______

42. During a lesson, an excellent way to ensure maximum retention of the material is to use:
    a. only lecture
    b. note taking
    c. student activities
    d. oral examination ______

43. The amount of information learned in an adult classroom is directly proportional to the amount of ________ the learners have.
    a. fun
    b. knowledge
    c. experience
    d. intelligence ______

44. The section of the lesson plan that allows the educator to provide an overview of the lesson is the:
    a. motivation and opening
    b. aims and objectives
    c. content in middle
    d. summary and review ______

45. A component that can be used to measure the learners' successes in achieving lesson objectives and assess the effectiveness of the teaching procedures is:
    a. analysis
    b. evaluation
    c. application
    d. comprehension ______

46. A master educator will use the lesson plans as a guide, but will reflect his or her uniqueness as an educator by:
    a. critiquing them
    b. analyzing them
    c. personalizing them
    d. reviewing them ______

47. Master educators will use their own history and experience to bring life and ________ into each class.
    a. information
    b. knowledge
    c. excitement
    d. analysis ______

48. Planning and developing a course of study is an individualized project that includes input from a wide range of ________.
    a. participants
    b. sources
    c. textbooks
    d. references ____

49. Planning considers the________, the school's facilities, the school's mission statement, course objectives, resources for course development, and more.
    a. extracurricular activities
    b. prescribed state curriculum
    c. product lines used
    d. school's ownership structure ____

50. A master educator will ________ and follow the curriculum and course of study established by the school without fail.
    a. disregard
    b. read
    c. respect
    d. critique ____

5 Developing and Using Educational Aids

1. Research in adult learning shows that ________ teaching is obsolete.
   a. learner-centered
   b. lecture-based
   c. hands-on
   d. nonprojected ____

2. Varying instructional materials and teaching aids encourages student ________ the material presented.
   a. interest in
   b. apathy toward
   c. lethargy toward
   d. confusion about ____

3. The average learner thinks at the rate of ________ words per minute.
   a. 200 to 300
   b. 300 to 400
   c. 400 to 500
   d. 500 to 600 ____

4. The average educator speaks at the rate of ________ words per minute.
   a. 110 to 160
   b. 160 to 210
   c. 210 to 300
   d. 70 to 110 ____

5. The more ________ the presentation can address, the greater the opportunity for understanding by the learner.
   a. emphasis
   b. variations
   c. emotions
   d. senses ____

6. A picture is three times more effective than words alone, and words and pictures are ________ times more effective than words alone.
   a. four
   b. five
   c. six
   d. seven ____

7. Well-prepared ________ can give a clearer meaning to words or directions that may otherwise be confusing.
   a. discussions c. instructions
   b. directions d. visual aids ____

8. Seventy-five percent of what a student learns is learned:
   a. by hearing c. by touching
   b. by seeing d. by tasting ____

9. Visual aids can be extremely helpful when teaching underlying theories, ________, and skills when it is not possible to bring actual circumstances into the classroom
   a. judgments c. emotions
   b. attitudes d. abilities ____

10. Visual aids used in conjunction with ________ will ensure that all key presentation points are covered in proper sequence.
    a. text materials c. lesson plans
    b. videotapes d. audiotapes ____

11. By using descriptive, clarifying teaching aids, there is less chance of the learner ________ the spoken word.
    a. hearing c. understanding
    b. misunderstanding d. missing ____

12. If some students have difficulty with reading or with the English language, visual aids should not be primarily of the ________ variety.
    a. three-dimensional c. chart
    b. photographic d. print ____

13. The master educator understands that the teaching materials and aids chosen will strongly ________ the degree of success achieved by the learners.
    a. decrease c. influence
    b. lessen d. counteract ____

14. A visual aid is hardly effective if it cannot be ________ by all learners.
    a. heard c. handled
    b. seen d. manipulated ____

15. An effective visual aid will explain a/an ________ concept or technique.
    a. important
    b. complex
    c. single
    d. convoluted ____

16. In depicting any physical technique or procedure in a visual aid, all parts should be in proper ________ to each other to avoid misleading the learner.
    a. proportion
    b. order
    c. arrangement
    d. sequencing ____

17. The use of colors in preparing visual aids will create learner ________.
    a. boredom
    b. lethargy
    c. anguish
    d. interest ____

18. The fundamental source of essential information is the:
    a. textbook
    b. workbook
    c. newspaper
    d. reference book ____

19. A tool used to complement the ________ and that allows for independent study is the workbook.
    a. textbook
    b. library
    c. newspaper
    d. references ____

20. Newspapers and trade magazine articles can be used effectively to give ________ and strength to text materials or information presented by the educator.
    a. color
    b. credibility
    c. eloquence
    d. cachet ____

21. Nonprojected visual aids include pictures, photographs, flip charts, bulletin boards, audiotapes, and:
    a. television
    b. computers
    c. chalkboards
    d. slides ____

22. Due to new technology, ________ are playing a much larger role in education.
    a. video recorders
    b. tape recorders
    c. overhead projectors
    d. computers ____

23. Audio instruction is presented primarily in the form of audio cassettes or compact discs, which are both convenient and ________.
   a. inexpensive
   b. costly
   c. irreplaceable
   d. ineffectual ____

24. Visual aids—pictures, photographs, charts, graphs, posters—are useful in presenting information in interesting ways that will enhance and ________ learning.
   a. stifle
   b. slow
   c. reduce
   d. motivate ____

25. Master educators may choose to use ________ to display a group of objects that are used to form an integrated whole for instructional purposes.
   a. electronics
   b. films
   c. videos
   d. exhibits ____

26. A more modern version of the chalkboard in common use today is the:
   a. blackboard
   b. bulletin board
   c. multipurpose board
   d. felt ____

27. An important procedure when using a chalkboard is to remember to speak to the ________.
   a. topic
   b. board
   c. issues
   d. learners ____

28. Generally, flip charts are suitable for a class of no more than ________ learners.
   a. 25 to 40
   b. 40 to 55
   c. 55 to 60
   d. 60 to 75 ____

29. A helpful hint when using flip charts is to use a variety of ________ that are not commonly used.
   a. related topics
   b. unrelated topics
   c. colored markers
   d. script letters ____

30. Using flip charts for ________ sessions allows learners to be involved while the educator still maintains control of the class.
   a. theory
   b. brainstorming
   c. practical
   d. testing ____

31. A new form of technology that uses bar-coding of information to allow for quick and easy access is called:
   a. CD-ROM image libraries
   b. laser disc imagery
   c. PowerPoint slides
   d. computerized overhead transparencies ______

32. One of the most commonly used methods of instructional materials in today's classroom is:
   a. video
   b. opaque projector
   c. laser discs
   d. computers ______

33. Because of ________, the individual classroom educator is no longer the sole facilitator of learning.
   a. CD-ROM image libraries
   b. laser disc imagery
   c. PowerPoint slides
   d. electronic delivery systems ______

34. ________ may be actual photographs that, when projected, appear more real than printed pictures because the colors are more brilliant.
   a. Slides
   b. Transparencies
   c. Overheads
   d. Filmstrips ______

35. A/An ________ presentation of a specific subject matter can often carry the bulk of the classroom presentation.
   a. charted
   b. graphed
   c. video
   d. audio ______

36. A helpful hint when using video education is to discourage ________ during the video.
   a. close observation
   b. note taking
   c. absolute silence
   d. close attention ______

37. ________ circuit television, which is primarily associated with the educational field, is a system through which the number of receiving units can be selectively controlled.
   a. Electronic
   b. Open
   c. Closed
   d. Visual ______

38. A projector that allows for projection of solid materials is a/an ________ projector.
   a. overhead
   b. opaque
   c. slide
   d. filmstrip ______

39. An advantage of using the overhead projector and transparencies is that they are:
   a. temporary c. versatile
   b. awkward d. expensive _____

40. The master educator will limit the number of ideas covered on only one transparency to _______.
   a. one c. three
   b. two d. four _____

41. When preparing transparencies, leave a space equal to the height of a/an _______ between each line.
   a. average letter c. lower-case letter
   b. upper-case letter d. script letter _____

42. If items listed on a transparency are _______, they should not be numbered but identified by bullets, characters, arrows, boxes, and so forth.
   a. sequential c. procedural
   b. related d. nonsequential _____

43. Never leave the overhead projector on a/an _______.
   a. important point c. metal table
   b. blank screen d. cloth cover _____

44. Audiovisual aids and projection equipment that is electronically powered must be handled with care and according to the _______ directions.
   a. manufacturer's c. supervisor's
   b. owner's d. verbal _____

45. The bottom of any viewing screen or board should be at least _______ inches from the floor, which will allow most learners to see the full screen clearly.
   a. 24 c. 36
   b. 32 d. 42 _____

46. For best viewing, the projection screen should be placed in a _______ at an angle facing the center of the room.
   a. back corner c. front corner
   b. side position d. centered position _____

47. A ________ surface should be used in a projection screen for greatest image visibility and seating breadth in the classroom.
    a. shiny
    b. slick
    c. rough
    d. matte ____

48. The distance from the projection screen to the last row of seats in a classroom should equal no more than ________ times the width of the screen.
    a. two
    b. four
    c. six
    d. eight ____

49. No row of seats should be ________ than its distance to the screen.
    a. narrower
    b. wider
    c. closer
    d. further ____

50. Master educators know that properly selected and effectively presented visual aids can add ________ and impact to his classroom.
    a. humor
    b. emotion
    c. sound
    d. power ____

6 Teaching Skills and Presentation Techniques

1. Neither efficiency nor intellect will serve educators well if they cannot ________ their knowledge and accomplishments to the learner.
   a. enforce
   b. communicate
   c. dictate
   d. moderate ______

2. To transmit information, thought, or feeling so that it is satisfactorily received or understood is known as:
   a. dictation
   b. hearing
   c. communication
   d. broadcasting ______

3. The challenge of communicating effectively with students is even greater because of the ________ backgrounds of today's adult learners.
   a. identical
   b. similar
   c. humble
   d. diverse ______

4. The generation that is typically considered to be defiant conformists, self-centered thinkers, and emotionally numb is:
   a. GI Joes
   b. baby boomers
   c. generation X
   d. generation Y ______

5. The generation that is considered to be rugged individualists and independent thinkers and who search for faith and meaning is:
   a. GI Joes
   b. baby boomers
   c. generation X
   d. generation Y ______

6. The generation that is considered to question racial categories, to value their parents' opinions, and to be more self-confident is:
   a. GI Joes
   b. baby boomers
   c. generation X
   d. generation Y ______

7. The generation that is always changing and responds well to print media is:
   a. GI Joes
   b. baby boomers
   c. generation X
   d. generation Y ____

8. Individuals born between 1946 and the early 1960s are generally considered to be:
   a. GI Joes
   b. baby boomers
   c. generation X
   d. generation Y ____

9. Baby boomers are on a quest for ________.
   a. physical security
   b. name notoriety
   c. substantial wealth
   d. spiritual security ____

10. As an educator you will allow your baby boomer students to provide input into ________ and will connect the information to their future career direction.
    a. lesson planning
    b. decision-making
    c. class scheduling
    d. curriculum development ____

11. Generation Xers are inclined to shirk ________ and are generally earning less money than their parents did at the same age.
    a. freedom
    b. independence
    c. money
    d. obligations ____

12. When teaching generation X, the master educator will encourage hope for them, nourish their imaginations, and focus on ________ rather than techniques.
    a. outcomes
    b. skills
    c. procedures
    d. rules ____

13. Research indicates that generation Y will tend to reject advertising that is targeted to ________.
    a. computer users
    b. single-parent households
    c. gender
    d. multicultural groups ____

14. Surveyed members of generation Y rated themselves as above average in leadership, popularity, ________, and social confidence.
    a. appearance
    b. attitude
    c. intellect
    d. communication ____

15. A master educator will increase awareness of a learner's culture and background by maintaining clear, ________ communication.
    a. limited
    b. reserved
    c. closed
    d. open ____

16. When teaching students whose first language is not your own, it is important to avoid ________.
    a. enunciation
    b. clarity
    c. intellect
    d. smiling ____

17. Behaviors and ________ change from culture to culture so it is necessary to be cautious in your interpretation of a learner's nonverbal messages.
    a. income
    b. emotions
    c. recreation
    d. mannerisms ____

18. When misunderstandings arise in a classroom of diverse learners, consider the possibility that they may be based on ________ perspectives or differences.
    a. cultural
    b. spiritual
    c. political
    d. attitudinal ____

19. As an educator, you will want to explain your own philosophy to learners from other cultures and encourage them to ask questions to obtain the ________ from their training.
    a. stated objectives
    b. maximum benefit
    c. minimum competency
    d. hours needed ____

20. The six Ps of education are referred to by the author of the *Master Educator* as:
    a. Proper Preparation and Presence Prevent Poor Performance
    b. Proper Preparation and Practice Promote Positive Performance
    c. Preliminary Preparation and Practice Promote Poor Performance
    d. Prior Preparation and Presence Prevent Positive Performance ____

21. After the lesson content has been identified, the first step in the building blocks that are the foundation of every good lesson or presentation is to:
    a. analyze your learners
    b. teach with poise
    c. be overly enthusiastic
    d. consider the topic ____

22. The second building block in the foundation of building a good lesson requires the educator to ________ and study additional reference materials.
    a. analyze learners
    b. conduct research
    c. properly prepare
    d. write tests ______

23. Throughout any presentation, a master educator will provide ________, which bring clarity and meaning to the points delivered.
    a. summaries
    b. adjectives
    c. examples
    d. warnings ______

24. The master educator must convey ________ in the classroom to have credibility with the learners.
    a. superiority and poise
    b. inflexibility and attitude
    c. respect and attitude
    d. poise and confidence ______

25. A master educator will believe in what she is saying and be ________ about it.
    a. enthusiastic
    b. autocratic
    c. vehement
    d. obstinate ______

26. A powerful presentation that enables learners to expand their skills, reinforce their ideals, and gain new knowledge will never occur if the learners are not ________.
    a. conversing
    b. reading
    c. listening
    d. talking ______

27. As human beings, adult learners need to feel a certain degree of control or ________ over others.
    a. subordination
    b. impotence
    c. subjugation
    d. mastery ______

28. Another need of human beings and adult learners is the need to enjoy ________ and a feeling of importance.
    a. vanity
    b. ego gratification
    c. conceit
    d. humility ______

29. Humans have a basic psychological need for ________.
    a. financial security
    b. mediocre achievement
    c. untold wealth
    d. financial precariousness ______

30. Adult learners must be reassured of their value and ________.
   a. triviality
   b. insignificance
   c. mediocrity
   d. worth ____

31. All human beings have an innate desire to have a sense of belonging and to ________.
   a. lose
   b. win
   c. draw
   d. fold ____

32. We all need the opportunity to express our creativity and feel we have contributed something ________.
   a. memorable
   b. inessential
   c. earth-shattering
   d. worthwhile ____

33. Even though motivation is internal, you as a master educator can create circumstances or situations by which your students can become ________.
   a. interested
   b. motivated
   c. lethargic
   d. provoked ____

34. An educator inspires learner motivation with strong personal contact; that is, arriving early for class and being available during ________ for personal discussion.
   a. breaks
   b. class
   c. lunch
   d. theory ____

35. Another method for instilling learner motivation is to get learners into a/an ________ mood.
   a. passive
   b. lazy
   c. active
   d. quiet ____

36. An educator should support course content with personal ________ to strengthen the objectives of the lesson.
   a. habits
   b. mannerisms
   c. history
   d. examples ____

37. A master educator will take care to avoid criticism of any type in a public situation or in front of peers and will recognize that praise is ________ when others hear it.
   a. bitter
   b. bleak
   c. sweeter
   d. factual ____

38. A master educator will encourage questions and learn how to address incorrect responses in a manner that does not _______ them.
    a. inspire
    b. encourage
    c. excite
    d. humiliate _____

39. A technique the educator can use to inspire learner motivation is to use good _______ during the presentation.
    a. eye contact
    b. personal grammar
    c. personal habits
    d. personal mannerisms _____

40. Identifying long-term _______ and stressing the value of internal motives will help your students understand the future advantage of mastering information or skills now.
    a. goals
    b. objectives
    c. targets
    d. benefits _____

41. Encouraging _______ among the learners will expand their network and support to ensure they get maximum benefit from the education provided.
    a. honesty
    b. reservations
    c. interaction
    d. privacy _____

42. By offering learners choices that they can make with respect to project completion or assignments, they feel that they have _______.
    a. futility
    b. control
    c. freedom
    d. importance _____

43. Studies show that _______ % of our communication is verbal (the words we use).
    a. 7
    b. 38
    c. 45
    d. 55 _____

44. Studies show that _______ % of our communication is visual (our overall appearance, body language, and gestures).
    a. 7
    b. 38
    c. 45
    d. 55 _____

45. Studies show that _______ % of our communication is vocal (how we speak our words).
    a. 7
    b. 38
    c. 45
    d. 55 _____

46. A/An ________ opening for your class informs learners that their time will be well used, that you understand who they are, and that you are well prepared for the class.
    a. irrelevant
    b. weak
    c. powerful
    d. eloquent _____

47. To hold the attention of the learner, the master educator must:
    a. present a dull attitude
    b. be enthusiastic and energetic
    c. present an uninterested attitude
    d. present an average appearance _____

48. Master educators place the focus on:
    a. the learners
    b. themselves
    c. the test
    d. the clock _____

49. The master educator will convey sincerity and interest with the learner by ________ eye contact.
    a. avoiding
    b. maintaining
    c. sporadic
    d. minimal _____

50. The structure of a lesson must be ________, simple to follow, and relevant to the needs of the learners.
    a. disparate
    b. antagonistic
    c. unrelated
    d. logical _____

51. The ________ structure for presentations allows the educator to present key points in a natural time sequence or historical order.
    a. problem/solution
    b. chronological
    c. topical
    d. spatial _____

52. The ________ structure for presentations is common when a challenge or problem is followed by a proposed solution.
    a. problem/solution
    b. challenge/solution
    c. challenge/answer
    d. theory/practice _____

53. The ________ structure for presentation allows the educator to list points in order of significance with the most important discussed at the beginning.
    a. spatial
    b. topical
    c. chronological
    d. challenge/solution _____

54. The ________ structure outlines the theory of a subject and then demonstrates how it works.
a. problem/solution
b. chronological
c. theory/practice
d. spatial ____

55. The ________ structure begins with general subject matter and progresses to more specific or vice versa.
a. challenge/answer
b. chronological
c. theory/practice
d. spatial ____

56. One method the master educator can use to strengthen the body or content of a lesson is to present:
a. facts and figures
b. examples and illustrations
c. anecdotes and analogies
d. a, b, and c ____

57. To make the most of a dynamic opening followed by well-prepared lesson content, it is important to end the class presentation ________.
a. by finishing on time
b. with no closing summary
c. with a powerful punch
d. by simply trailing off ____

58. The master educator will summarize the general lesson, restate the key points, and then present the learners with a/an ________ for action or performance.
a. directive
b. challenge
c. encouragement
d. recommendation ____

59. An important element of bringing a presentation to closure includes the educator's responsibility to ________ student learning and progress.
a. evaluate
b. estimate
c. calculate
d. question ____

60. When moving from one part of a lesson to another, the master educator will want to ________ all the parts through transitions.
a. disconnect
b. separate
c. connect
d. distract ____

61. Techniques such as pausing, Q & A, physical activity or movement, visual aids, or redirecting attention, which bring all the parts of a lesson together, are called ________.
a. connectors
b. attachers
c. connections
d. transitions ____

62. Adult learners can listen with understanding for 90 minutes, but can only listen with retention for ________ minutes.
    a. 10 c. 30
    b. 20 d. 40 _____

63. Form of varying the stimuli by speaking with the whole body is called using:
    a. exercises c. energizers
    b. activities d. gestures _____

64. A master educator will learn to use her ________ to create excitement and enthusiasm.
    a. history c. voice
    b. dress d. vocabulary _____

65. Using a "shocking" opening statement is known as a/an ________.
    a. attention grabber c. mind setter
    b. attention seeker d. mind-boggler _____

66. Master educators will use energizers and stress relievers at a point when the class needs a lift or change of ________.
    a. direction c. topic
    b. attitude d. pace _____

67. Changing pace is to switch from a/an ________ teaching method to a/an ________ teaching method.
    a. lecture/discussion c. mind mapping/window paning
    b. oral/visual d. demonstration/role play _____

68. Questions will generally elicit information or ________ on a variety of topics, which should go from general to specific.
    a. attitudes c. opinions
    b. emotions d. doubts _____

69. Effective ________ is an important part of answering questions.
    a. gesturing c. movements
    b. voice d. listening _____

70. Two different types of questions are low-order or ________ questions and high order questions.
    a. true/false c. recall
    b. completion d. application _____

71. Three methods for questioning are group questioning, direct questioning, and:
   a. indirect questioning c. redirect questioning
   b. straightforward questioning d. individual questioning _____

72. The master educator must be prepared to give ________ reinforcement to students throughout the educational process.
   a. negative c. indirect
   b. positive d. contrary _____

7 Results-Oriented Classroom Management

1. The goal of every master educator should be to create a/an ________ learning environment that will provide a pathway to career success for students.
   a. entertaining c. negative
   b. positive d. hip ____

2. The educator of the 21st century is better known as a ________ of learning rather than a teacher.
   a. director c. facilitator
   b. manager d. leader ____

3. The educator's image, attitude, and actions are often ________ by the learners' behavior.
   a. mirrored c. critiqued
   b. rejected d. ridiculed ____

4. By establishing ________, the master educator will be more effective at maintaining order and control in the classroom.
   a. friendship and authority c. intimacy and credibility
   b. friendship and credibility d. credibility and authority ____

5. Learners will react more favorably and desired behaviors can be shaped more quickly and permanently through ________ means than through aversive ones.
   a. negative c. positive
   b. friendly d. indifferent ____

6. In maintaining good discipline in the classroom, the method that uses the least amount of force is considered:
   a. high-profile intervention c. low-profile intervention
   b. uniformity and consistency d. high interactive conferencing ____

7. In maintaining good discipline in the classroom, the method that requires more force and requires more time and effort is the ________ method.
   a. high-profile intervention
   b. uniformity and consistency
   c. low-profile intervention
   d. ignore and proceed ____

8. Low-profile techniques that can be used in the classroom to help minimize disruptive behavior include ignoring it, eye contact, verbal desists, and:
   a. threatening
   b. reprimands
   c. conferences
   d. name dropping ____

9. The low-profile technique that involves the use of a verbal cue or command to stop the behavior is called:
   a. name dropping
   b. close proximity
   c. verbal desist
   d. eye contact ____

10. A powerful means of controlling misbehavior is to ________ the learner who is in violation.
    a. physically move toward
    b. take questions from
    c. avoid looking at
    d. take action against ____

11. Eye contact can be used with little effort on the part of the educator and can be a powerful control strategy for ________ misconduct.
    a. major
    b. chronic
    c. minor
    d. deliberate ____

12. The secondary purpose of using behavior control procedures is to permanently ________ misconduct.
    a. eliminate
    b. increase
    c. delineate
    d. identify ____

13. A high-profile intervention method that is common and can be applied both publicly and privately, depending on the circumstances, is ________.
    a. praise
    b. reprimands
    c. agreements
    d. conferences ____

14. A high-profile intervention method that involves a private meeting between the educator and the learner is ________.
    a. praise
    b. reprimands
    c. eye contact
    d. conferences ____

15. If it is determined that the established consequences are not effective and do not work in resolving rule violations, they should be ________.
   a. reinforced
   b. explained
   c. changed
   d. ignored
   _____

16. A/An ________ contract will add meaning to an agreement made between the educator and learner.
   a. verbal
   b. intended
   c. implied
   d. written
   _____

17. Anyone or anything that prevents students from achieving the learning objective is considered a:
   a. knowledge barrier
   b. learning barrier
   c. situational barrier
   d. chronic barrier
   _____

18. When a learner behaves in a difficult manner consistently and affects other learners in an uncomfortable way, it is a:
   a. knowledge barrier
   b. learning barrier
   c. situational barrier
   d. chronic barrier
   _____

19. When a learner temporarily exhibits "difficult" behavior that is different from the personality or behavior usually exhibited, it is a:
   a. learning environment
   b. learning barrier
   c. situational barrier
   d. chronic barrier
   _____

20. Effective ________ is critical in dealing with the various obstacles to learning.
   a. discipline
   b. communication
   c. listening
   d. speech
   _____

21. One strategy that has proved effective in dealing with the student who constantly seeks the educator's attention is to use the ________ message.
   a. verbal
   b. critical
   c. unspoken
   d. physical
   _____

22. A strategy that can be effective in dealing with the constant attention seeker is to assign the less interesting ________ to the learner.
   a. clients
   b. mannequins
   c. chapters
   d. projects
   _____

23. One method that has been effectively used by educators to minimize chronic tardiness is to give a __________ to those who arrive on time.
    a. warm breakfast
    b. gift certificate
    c. heartfelt thanks
    d. severe reprimand _____

24. Beginning a class late to accommodate latecomers rewards ________ performers and penalizes those who are on time.
    a. poor
    b. prompt
    c. committed
    d. dedicated _____

25. One solution for encouraging prompt attendance is giving a token reward to the first learner who provides a solution to the ________ race.
    a. marathon
    b. relay
    c. riddle
    d. class _____

26. Involving the chronic latecomer in the process of keeping ________ for the class will help her become more prompt.
    a. grades
    b. projects
    c. breaks
    d. time _____

27. You can recognize a learner who is too shy to participate by his lack of ________ and passive attitude.
    a. energy
    b. indolence
    c. weakness
    d. idleness _____

28. One strategy used effectively with shy learners is to use small groups and ________ the leadership role.
    a. assign
    b. dictate
    c. rotate
    d. eliminate _____

29. A behavior that can be disconcerting and harmful to the education process is ________ in class.
    a. participating
    b. sleeping
    c. involvement
    d. discussion _____

30. An effective strategy in dealing with learners who nod off in class is to engage a/an ________.
    a. energizer
    b. drug
    c. lecture
    d. attorney _____

31. Learners who are constantly engaged in side conversations tend to try to ________ discussions in the classroom.
a. control c. lead
b. monopolize d. minimize ______

32. One strategy that can be used in dealing with students who are constantly engaged in side conversations is to stop your ________.
a. delivery c. intonation
b. breathing d. variation ______

33. You might recognize the chronic ________ by her negative body language and her constant argument that what you are suggesting will never work.
a. optimist c. lazybones
b. philanthropist d. pessimist ______

34. When faced with the inevitable statement that your theories will not work, ask the student to ________.
a. leave class c. stay late
b. explain why d. do sanitation ______

35. A strategy that has been effective in dealing with negative attitudes about your procedures is to obtain ________ from prior learners.
a. letters c. testimonials
b. photos d. anecdotes ______

36. Inattentiveness and preoccupation can be recognized when the learner appears to be in outer space or involved in other ________.
a. learning c. energizers
b. activities d. education ______

37. One method for dealing with the preoccupied learner is to have all students make a list of all their ________ at the beginning of the class and then put it away for later reference.
a. monthly bills c. pending activities
b. family members d. personal desires ______

38. The challenge faced with a student who appears to "know it all" is that the enthusiasm and overt participation can ________ the participation of other learners.
a. encourage c. enhance
b. squelch d. maximize ______

39. One strategy for dealing with the learner who acts if he has all the answers is to open the class with a/an ________ exercise.
   a. impossible　　c. irrelevant
   b. relevant　　d. physical　　_____

40. The chronic ________ is one who wants to share his personal experiences on every matter and who takes lots longer to get a point across than most other learners.
   a. complainer　　c. interrupter
   b. speaker　　d. narrator　　_____

41. An effective strategy for dealing with frequent interruptions in class is to limit each learner's response by having her place her hand in a ________ and allow them to talk only until she has to remove her hand.
   a. boiling hot water　　c. pot of sand
   b. bucket of ice　　d. jar of bugs　　_____

42. The educator and learner should agree on a plan of action to improve areas that are not ________.
   a. relevant　　c. satisfactory
   b. academic　　d. practical　　_____

43. It is important for the master educator to give regular and thorough ________ to students regarding their achievements.
   a. criticism　　c. punishment
   b. discipline　　d. feedback　　_____

44. When conducting a counseling session with a student, it should be held in:
   a. public　　c. class
   b. private　　d. clinic　　_____

45. The classroom arrangement suitable for roundtable-type discussions is the ________ arrangement.
   a. semicircle　　c. chevron style
   b. boardroom　　d. U-shaped table　　_____

46. The classroom arrangement that is effective for learner-centered education and can accommodate the use of projected visual aids is the ________ arrangement.
   a. half-rounds/crescents　　c. chevron style
   b. boardroom　　d. U-shaped table　　_____

47. The style of seating that is also known as the V-shape and allows for good eye contact among learners is the ________ arrangement.
    a. semicircle
    b. boardroom
    c. chevron style
    d. U-shaped table ______

48. The classroom style that is highly effective for small classes up to 10 learners and ensures good interaction among students is the ________ arrangement.
    a. semicircle
    b. boardroom
    c. chevron style
    d. U-shaped table ______

49. Administrative responsibilities an instructor may be responsible for include daily lesson plans, inventory and requisitions, and ________.
    a. financial aid
    b. student hours
    c. student recruitment
    d. monthly payroll ______

50. Master educators inform students of what to expect and they make themselves available to students to discuss issues of importance and relevance to the learner's ________.
    a. attitude
    b. emotions
    c. progress
    d. stagnation ______

8 Industry Needs

1. New salon professionals are as responsible for ________ as the seasoned professionals already on board.
   a. overall salon growth
   b. advertising and promotions
   c. management and operations
   d. personnel performance evaluations _____

2. In addition to technical abilities, salon owners indicate that new licensees should also be able to communicate with clients, understand business operations, have a strong desire for success, and have a/an ________ the industry.
   a. interest in
   b. passion for
   c. affinity for
   d. kinship with _____

3. Master educators will avail themselves of the educational materials and ________ that will put their students on a par with the needs of the salons that will be competing for their employment.
   a. products
   b. equipment
   c. technology
   d. texts _____

4. Master educators will be open to ideas, eager to ________, focused on the learner, and aware of the industry and its needs.
   a. speak
   b. listen
   c. communicate
   d. observe _____

5. Surveyed salons indicate that they want to hire graduates who have a sound ________ of all the basics.
   a. familiarity
   b. knowledge
   c. awareness
   d. mastery _____

6. Master educators will help their students develop their own ________ sense of design and styling as they consult with the clients daily.
   a. extraneous
   b. trained
   c. intuitive
   d. common
   _____

7. With the geometric cut revolution of the 1960s, created by ________, precision hair-cutting techniques and craftsmanship became essential.
   a. Vidal Sassoon
   b. Paul Mitchell
   c. N. F. Cimaglia
   d. Estee Lauder
   _____

8. Salons indicate that new graduates should be able to complete a consultation and haircut in:
   a. 30 minutes
   b. 45 minutes
   c. 1 hour
   d. 1-1/2 hours
   _____

9. Salons indicate that many new licensees fail to "complete" the haircut by checking the ________ and making sure the cut is appropriately blended.
   a. guide
   b. partings
   c. perimeter
   d. nape
   _____

10. Once barber or cosmetology students have mastered the essentials of haircutting, they can then add creative ________ to make every haircut an individual work of art.
    a. lines
    b. color
    c. sensitivity
    d. flair
    _____

11. The master educator will make certain that barber and cosmetology students understand the endless possibilities for ________ in hairstyling.
    a. shape and design
    b. length and volume
    c. texture and length
    d. volume and texture
    _____

12. Master educators should prepare barber and cosmetology graduates with the ability to perform the style consultation and service within ________.
    a. 15 minutes
    b. 30 minutes
    c. 45 minutes
    d. 1 hour
    _____

13. The visual or tactile surface characteristics and appearance of something, including hair, is known as:
    a. density
    b. porosity
    c. texture
    d. color
    _____

14. A new term used to replace older terms such as *perms*, *permanent waves*, and *chemical reformation* is:
    a. texture perms
    b. chemical waves
    c. perm services
    d. texture services ____

15. One of the most frequent requests that clients for hair services have is ________.
    a. bright color
    b. pin-curl styling
    c. hair manageability
    d. bouffant styling ____

16. Salon surveys indicate that a new employee should be able to perform a texture service in:
    a. 30 minutes
    b. 45 minutes
    c. 90 minutes
    d. 2 hours ____

17. What service is viewed as the "cosmetic" for hair?
    a. texture services
    b. colors
    c. haircuts
    d. styles ____

18. Salons are looking for employees who know how to make a color decision with a client have the ________ to complete a quality service.
    a. attitude
    b. desire
    c. skills
    d. interest ____

19. A student who specializes in skin care, rather than hair is called a/an:
    a. electrologist
    b. esthetician
    c. aromatherapist
    d. manicurist ____

20. The application of artificial nails or nail extensions was introduced in:
    a. early 20th century
    b. late 20th century
    c. middle 20th century
    d. early 21st century ____

21. Technology has resulted in a wide variety of methods for ________ and lengthening natural nails.
    a. thickening
    b. weakening
    c. strengthening
    d. damaging ____

22. If electrology is the chosen field, research indicates that new employees should be highly skilled and conscious of ________ and infection control.
    a. safety measures
    b. removal techniques
    c. insertion methods
    d. body hair ____

23. Entry level electrologists must have mastered the selection of the proper needle, the intensity and timing of the current used, and the ________ and depth of insertion of the needle.
    a. attitude
    b. angle
    c. frequency
    d. pain ____

24. Massage therapy is widely recognized as an effective means of reducing the incidence of ________ disorders and relieving soft-tissue pain and dysfunction.
    a. sore muscle
    b. weak back
    c. stress-related
    d. attention deficit ____

25. Massage therapists need to be able to demonstrate knowledge of basic ________ as a requisite for mastering the theory and practice of therapeutic body massage.
    a. human body and mind
    b. human skeleton and muscles
    c. physical and mental attitudes
    d. human anatomy and physiology ____

26. When analyzing a budget, the most expensive area in salon operations is:
    a. rent
    b. payroll
    c. supplies
    d. utilities ____

27. The successful salon should generate a profit margin of:
    a. 5% to 10%
    b. 10% to 15%
    c. 15% to 20%
    d. 20% to 25% ____

28. At the top of the list of characteristics sought in new employees, salon owners indicate the critical importance of effective ________.
    a. management skills
    b. delegation skills
    c. communication skills
    d. time management ____

29. The client ________ begins in the first few seconds, during the greeting.
    a. service
    b. connection
    c. introduction
    d. consultation ____

30. When a stylist wants to understand a client's perceptions, ideas, and feelings, she should ask ________ questions.
    a. open-ended
    b. yes/no
    c. closed-ended
    d. unrelated ____

31. When a stylist is looking for facts such as where the client works or how often she shampoos her hair, she should ask ________ questions.
   a. open-ended
   b. yes/no
   c. closed-ended
   d. unrelated
   _____

32. Once the asking part of the connection with a salon client has been established, the ________ part of the connection begins.
   a. teaching
   b. conversation
   c. talking
   d. consultation
   _____

33. Salon employees should be not only skilled in successful consultations but also in confirming their ________ of what the client has answered.
   a. interest
   b. understanding
   c. explanation
   d. opinion
   _____

34. Of utmost interest to salons is the ability in new employees to develop a ________.
   a. client database
   b. client birthday list
   c. client service plan
   d. client reminder card
   _____

35. It is the responsibility of the master educator to communicate with area employers to determine their current needs and expectations so she can prepare graduates for ________.
   a. course completion
   b. extracurricular activities
   c. student competitions
   d. successful employment
   _____

9 Teaching in a Dynamic Clinic

1. The ultimate success of any cosmetology school may relate to how successfully the ________ is managed and supervised.
   a. classroom
   b. advertising
   c. clinic
   d. business
   _____

2. The transition from school to the salon is made easier for students who experience ________ training.
   a. reception desk
   b. "real world"
   c. classroom practical
   d. classroom theory
   _____

3. The master educator should ensure that the clinic is a/an ________, well-managed, and highly supervised training environment.
   a. calm
   b. indifferent
   c. moderate
   d. exciting
   _____

4. The more revenue that can be generated in the clinic or laboratory, the greater the potential for a/an ________ in the overall cost of student tuition.
   a. offset
   b. increase
   c. addition
   d. propagation
   _____

5. According to surveys, what percentage of students' success comes from their people skills?
   a. 50
   b. 60
   c. 70
   d. 80
   _____

6. Students may practice their people skills and communication skills by training ________.
   a. in the classroom
   b. on the mannequins
   c. in the clinic
   d. in theory class
   _____

7. Students should be taught from the very beginning of their course of study that their success as students in ________ will determine their entry-level success in the salon.
   a. the classroom
   b. mannequin practice
   c. the clinic
   d. technical skills _____

8. Your role as a master educator is to teach your students ________ habits and behavior that will serve them well as professionals.
   a. insipid
   b. decadent
   c. disconcerting
   d. success _____

9. Research indicates that for optimum profit, schools should attempt to generate ________, which represents at least 50% of the overall operating income.
   a. retail sales
   b. clinic revenue
   c. book sales
   d. student sales _____

10. Schools should expect a minimum net profit of ________ %.
    a. 5
    b. 10
    c. 15
    d. 20 _____

11. Student tuition collections should represent ________ % of the overall operating income.
    a. 20
    b. 30
    c. 40
    d. 50 _____

12. What percentage of the clinic revenue should be derived from retail sales?
    a. 10
    b. 15
    c. 25
    d. 50 _____

13. Master educators will make sure that the clinic experience is a/an ________ for the students.
    a. adventure
    b. safari
    c. choice
    d. passive _____

14. Students should be taught from the very beginning of their training that their assignment is to graduate but their ________ is to develop a solid client base.
    a. only purpose
    b. primary purpose
    c. short-term goal
    d. long-term goal _____

15. Science shows that positive self-suggestion and ________ are highly effective in helping anyone achieve important life goals.
    a. imagination
    b. materialization
    c. visualization
    d. consideration ____

16. The ability to work together toward a common vision is known as:
    a. autonomy
    b. association
    c. teamwork
    d. unity ____

17. Part of the students' role on the school team is to develop a sound client base and generate ________, which contributes to the overall success of the institution.
    a. clinic revenue
    b. public relations
    c. book sales
    d. effective sanitation ____

18. One role of the master educator as a member of the school team is to impart ________ and facilitate learning for all students through teaching, grading, coaching, and mentoring.
    a. personal history
    b. sound education
    c. friendly relations
    d. indifferent attitudes ____

19. One goal in building a profitable clinic is for each student to develop a sound, annual client base of at least ________ clients.
    a. 150
    b. 250
    c. 300
    d. 500 ____

20. Sometimes team members attempt to put responsibility on the shoulders of another team member. But if a common vision and goals are shared, common ________ should also be shared.
    a. ideals
    b. attitudes
    c. feelings
    d. responsibilities ____

21. When the entire school team focuses on the common goal of higher clinic revenue, ________ is increased, educational quality improves, and everyone benefits.
    a. profit
    b. absenteeism
    c. injury
    d. indebtedness ____

22. A dirty or disorderly reception area or clinic can seriously ________ a community's image of the institution and the education it provides.
    a. enhance
    b. tarnish
    c. strengthen
    d. intensify ____

23. The committed school team will ensure that the facility and equipment are monitored ________ and needed repairs are reported to appropriate school personnel as quickly as possible.
    a. regularly
    b. sporadically
    c. monthly
    d. annually _____

24. The school team member, whether a student, educator, or administrative personnel, should automatically take steps to ________ minor image concerns that need improvement.
    a. report
    b. ignore
    c. list
    d. correct _____

25. The challenge and opportunity of operating the ________ is one of the most important jobs in the operation of a school or professional establishment.
    a. theory classroom
    b. admissions office
    c. reception desk
    d. inventory control _____

26. The reception area is the first thing clients and prospective students see when they arrive at the school, and their perception should be ________.
    a. a negative one
    b. a positive one
    c. one of indifference
    d. one of concern _____

27. Items that should be readily available at the reception desk are the appointment book, client tickets, record cards, and ________.
    a. chemical release forms
    b. back bar products
    c. theory lesson plans
    d. student education files _____

28. It is ________ to assign a client to a student is who is attending a scheduled theory class.
    a. acceptable
    b. routine
    c. unacceptable
    d. encouraged _____

29. In schools of cosmetology what form is designed to release the school and students from responsibility for accidents or damages?
    a. client record card
    b. incident report form
    c. hold harmless form
    d. change of address _____

30. Master educators will ensure that all students understand the criticality of obtaining the client's signature on a release statement ________.
    a. during the service
    b. after the service
    c. when paying bill
    d. prior to service _____

31. A completed client record card should contain hair analysis notes, strand tests, timing, ________, and suggestions for the next service.
 a. blouse/shirt color c. service results
 b. child's birthday d. client signature _____

32. Accurate client records are also important to ________ who may be providing different services to the client either on the same day or at another time.
 a. other clinic/salon personnel c. the admissions director
 b. reception desk attendant d. the school administrator _____

33. The dispensary of a school should contain back bar products needed daily and ________ that may not be included in student kits.
 a. tools and implements c. hold harmless cards
 b. client record cards d. long hair mannequins _____

34. Responsibilities of the dispensary attendant include keeping the back bar shampoo and conditioning rinse replenished and changing the ________ as directed.
 a. sanitation duty roster c. disinfectant soak solution
 b. inventory control procedures d. school's maintenance schedule _____

35. A key to developing a loyal customer is the ________ they receive from their student stylist.
 a. complacency c. indifference
 b. greeting d. suggestions _____

36. When a student stylist comes to the reception area to greet the next client, the student should be ________.
 a. rushed c. serious
 b. smiling d. indifferent _____

37. Institutions are encouraged to develop methods that acknowledge ________ clients and make them feel special, appreciated, important, and welcome.
 a. return c. referred
 b. repeat d. first-time _____

38. On completion of the service for any client, students should escort the client back to the reception area, offer to book the next appointment, and suggest ________.
 a. a nice tip c. an add-on service
 b. applicable retail products d. they come on time _____

39. ________ services refer to the client who returns every 4 to 6 weeks for a service but does not necessarily schedule the next appointment before leaving the facility.
   a. Rebook
   b. Repeat
   c. Advance
   d. Preliminary ______

40. One method for building a solid clientele, whether in school or in the salon, is to obtain ________ from clients.
   a. tips
   b. cards
   c. referrals
   d. repeats ______

41. Students should be taught to be ________ in the client referral activity.
   a. persistent
   b. consistent
   c. reticent
   d. indignant ______

42. Students should hand out three business cards to clients and ask for referrals of their friends, neighbors, associates, and relatives every ________ visit.
   a. second to third
   b. third to fourth
   c. fourth to fifth
   d. fifth to sixth ______

43. Master educators might suggest that students develop a ________ for client development.
   a. written plan
   b. verbal plan
   c. recorded message
   d. sincere attempt ______

44. Ticket upgrading, also known as "add-ons," is another method for increasing ________.
   a. book sales
   b. clinic revenue
   c. tuition revenue
   d. kit sales ______

45. Professional ________ mandate that the student stylist does not suggest services or products that are not needed by the client.
   a. regulations
   b. oversight
   c. ethics
   d. authorities ______

46. Getting students involved in developing promotions for special occasions relates with their ________ training.
   a. people skills
   b. technical skills
   c. business skills
   d. theory class ______

47. For a clinic to be considered dynamic, there really should be no _______ for student stylists.
a. downtime
b. scheduled appointments
c. busy season
d. personal requests _____

48. A card that is mailed out to the institution's or salon's regular client list to let them know about special promotions or events is a/an _______.
a. client appreciation card
b. client referral card
c. chemical reminder card
d. client awareness card _____

49. A card sent to regular clients that simply explains how much their loyal patronage is appreciated is a _______.
a. client appreciation card
b. client referral card
c. chemical reminder card
d. client awareness card _____

50. A general mailing to every client in the school or salon's record file system is considered _______.
a. contacting inactive clients
b. general client campaign
c. sending reminder notes
d. client referral cards _____

51. Research shows that stylists only spend approximately _______ % of their time actually serving clients.
a. 50
b. 60
c. 70
d. 80 _____

52. The first thing a client will notice about a student is her _______.
a. attitude
b. image
c. personality
d. religion _____

53. Master educators know that a willingness to _______ is a key ingredient to success.
a. gossip frequently
b. play occasionally
c. work hard
d. procrastinate regularly _____

54. Students must understand that their clients are human beings who need _______ and being made to feel special.
a. discountenance
b. pampering
c. suppression
d. chastening _____

55. When students develop an enthusiasm for getting the job done, that enthusiasm will become _______.
a. annoying
b. contagious
c. bothersome
d. inconvenient _____

56. Students should be taught to ________ when they are interacting with clients.
a. extend themselves
b. discuss themselves
c. discuss religion
d. discuss politics _____

57. Master educators will encourage students to begin their ________ when they are first assigned to the clinic.
a. job hunting
b. professional resumé
c. professional portfolio
d. salon search _____

58. When a clinic floor educator or supervisor is assigned to a specific number of stations and students for which he is responsible, it is called ________.
a. area teaching
b. zone teaching
c. one-on-one teaching
d. proactive teaching _____

59. The first step in zone teaching requires the educator to walk through the area or zone and check for ________.
a. comfort
b. attitudes
c. safety
d. product _____

60. The second step in zone teaching requires the educator to walk through and check the area for ________.
a. comfort
b. attitudes
c. safety
d. product _____

61. The third element in zone teaching requires the educator to ________.
a. take a break
b. teach the students
c. supervise the clients
d. style client's hair _____

62. Master educators will teach students to check their own haircuts by using partings that are ________ those used when performing the actual cut.
a. the same as
b. larger than
c. opposite to
d. smaller than _____

63. To prevent a dissatisfied client, the educator must make ________ rounds through the clinic, teaching in a pattern of student-to-student.
a. frequent
b. infrequent
c. sporadic
d. occasional _____

64. Keeping unsightly haircolor stains off clinic floors is the responsibility of the ________.
a. owners
b. students
c. clients
d. educators ____

65. Master educators will plan for demonstrations in the clinic by having their own ________.
a. kit of implements
b. drape and towels
c. platform and microphone
d. written demonstration schedule ____

66. To openly criticize a student's work in front of a client causes humiliation and embarrassment, and nothing contributes more to a ________ student than such behavior.
a. happy
b. satisfied
c. complacent
d. dropped ____

67. Master educators must assume a large role in ensuring that the clinic is maintained in a ________ manner at all times.
a. busy and cluttered
b. clean and safe
c. normal, disorderly
d. professional and unsanitary ____

68. Educators who assume that such menial tasks as washing and folding towels are beneath them will never achieve the status of ________.
a. time clock operator
b. evening receptionist
c. master educator
d. front door monitor ____

69. When a master educator has developed a dynamic clinic, she will have generated a spirit of ________ that will carry to every client who enters the clinic.
a. enthusiasm
b. indifference
c. apathy
d. lethargy ____

70. ________ activities are far more effective at promoting the clinic than spending hard dollars on planned advertising.
a. Telethon
b. Community service
c. Parents' day
d. Extracurricular ____

10 Student Evaluation and Testing Methods

1. One purpose of grading is to encourage learner ________ and to build learner confidence.
   a. complacency
   b. emotion
   c. achievement
   d. anxiety
   _____

2. One purpose of grading is to identify educational progress and measure the ________, skill, and attitude of the learners.
   a. ability
   b. knowledge
   c. emotion
   d. complacency
   _____

3. It is essential for an educator to become proficient in ________ the knowledge acquired by the learner.
   a. measuring
   b. criticizing
   c. belittling
   d. brandishing
   _____

4. When a student receives a good grade from the educator, it provides the student positive reinforcement and builds ________.
   a. client base
   b. self-confidence
   c. portfolio
   d. skills
   _____

5. The educator must measure how far the learner has come to plan for her ________.
   a. career success
   b. exam preparation
   c. future training
   d. life's work
   _____

6. Master educators will use grading to ________ learners and assess their progress rather than to trick them.
   a. challenge
   b. harass
   c. mollify
   d. appease
   _____

7. Learners will be motivated to improve their performance if they believe the grading procedures are ________.
   a. partial
   b. easy
   c. critical
   d. fair
   _____

8. The grading policies and procedures must correlate with the ________ objectives to be effective.
   a. student
   b. educational
   c. educator
   d. career
   _____

9. The three categories of performance that are usually assessed in schools of cosmetology and related fields are theoretical knowledge, practical skills, and ________.
   a. emotion
   b. complacency
   c. attitude
   d. anxiety
   _____

10. Theoretical knowledge is assessed through written tests consisting of true and false, completion, multiple choice, matching exercise, and ________ questions.
    a. survey
    b. essay
    c. opinion
    d. attitude
    _____

11. Practical skills may be assessed using ________ evaluation methods such as the Likert Scale, the rating scale, checklists, and performance checklists.
    a. survey
    b. attitude
    c. performance
    d. opinion
    _____

12. When a method of grading does not involve the cooperation of the learner, it is considered to be ________ centered.
    a. learner
    b. student
    c. client
    d. teacher
    _____

13. ________ evaluation is that which determines what the student knows after having been taught certain material or skills.
    a. Outcome
    b. Summative
    c. Consequence
    d. Practical
    _____

14. ________ evaluation is the process of assigning grades after testing has occurred.
    a. Outcome
    b. Summative
    c. Consequence
    d. Practical
    _____

15. Giving grades according to the mood of the educator at the time of grading has been called ________.
    a. grading with spite c. grading by disposition
    b. grading without risk d. grading by assumption _____

16. Giving low grades to a particular learner because he is not liked by the educator has been called ________.
    a. grading with spite c. grading by disposition
    b. grading without risk d. grading by assumption _____

17. When educators always give average grades to every learner to remain on safe ground, it may be called ________.
    a. grading with spite c. grading by disposition
    b. grading without risk d. grading by assumption _____

18. When the educator always targets one detail or skill behavior to grade down for all learners, it is known as ________.
    a. grading with warm fuzzies c. grading by personal fetish
    b. grading with spite d. grading improvement only _____

19. When the educator unconsciously gives learners either higher or lower scores based on previous performance by the learner, it is known as ________.
    a. grading with warm fuzzies c. grading by personal fetish
    b. grading by assumption d. grading improvement only _____

20. When an educator gives grades for work he has not actually seen performed, it is known as ________.
    a. grading in absentia c. grading by personal fetish
    b. grading with warm fuzzies d. grading improvement only _____

21. Testing is the most ________ method for measuring knowledge.
    a. proficient c. menial
    b. ineffective d. mediocre _____

22. After determining relevant and important test content, educators must establish a ________.
    a. test schedule c. test list
    b. test review d. test plan _____

23. Educators must determine the importance of each content area of a test by a process referred to as ________.
    a. selection
    b. balancing
    c. weighting
    d. comparison _____

24. ________ tests are those that can be completed by at least 80% of the students within 1 hour.
    a. Difficult
    b. Power
    c. Essay
    d. Easy _____

25. The test format that allows the educator to develop a large number of questions and the learner to answer a large number of questions in a short period of time is called ________.
    a. true and false
    b. multiple choice
    c. essay
    d. fill in the blank _____

26. In ________ questioning, the student may place into long-term memory the incorrect information or statement for recall at a future time.
    a. true and false
    b. multiple choice
    c. essay
    d. fill in the blank _____

27. When writing ________ test items, it is important to avoid the use of the words *not*, *usually*, *always*, and *never*.
    a. multiple choice
    b. essay
    c. matching
    d. true and false _____

28. Questions that are used to test the students' precise recall, associations, and discriminations within their memory are ________ questions.
    a. multiple choice
    b. essay
    c. matching
    d. fill in the blank _____

29. One important guideline to remember when writing matching items for testing is to keep all items and possible matches ________.
    a. equal in length
    b. on the same page
    c. uncommon to each other
    d. designed to trick learners _____

30. Questions that require the learner to provide an answer in either sentence, paragraph, or short composition format are known as ________ questions.
    a. true and false
    b. matching
    c. multiple choice
    d. essay _____

31. ________ questions are used to determine the learner's knowledge, comprehension level, and ability to analyze information and apply it properly in a practical situation.
a. Essay
b. Matching
c. Fill in the blank
d. True and false ____

32. To eliminate some of the subjectivity involved in scoring essay test questions, the educator should first write a/an ________.
a. outline of the test
b. response to each question
c. objective for the question
d. definition for each question ____

33. When writing completion items, the questions or statements must be prepared in such a manner that there is/are ________ correct answer(s).
a. one
b. two
c. three
d. four ____

34. One hint to remember when writing completion test items is to keep each item as ________ as possible.
a. long
b. short
c. elaborate
d. rambling ____

35. In multiple choice questions, the possible answers that are incorrect are known as ________.
a. attractors
b. advancers
c. foils
d. checkers ____

36. An advantage of multiple choice test questions is that they are ________ in scoring, which increases agreement among educators as to the correct answer.
a. objective
b. subjective
c. biased
d. opinionated ____

37. When writing multiple choice test questions, the stem should be stated in the ________.
a. negative
b. subjective
c. affirmative
d. assertive ____

38. The grading method that encourages educators to observe student behaviors in a natural environment using a systematic, 5-point scoring scale is the ________.
a. rating scale
b. Likert scale
c. performance checklist
d. checklist ____

39. The grading method used to compare a student's performance or behavior with specific standards or criteria established for a designated learning category is the ________.
a. rating scale
b. Likert scale
c. performance checklist
d. checklist ____

40. A variation of the rating scale method of grading that uses fewer rating categories is known as the ________.
a. rating scale
b. Likert scale
c. performance checklist
d. checklist ____

41. The grading method that master educators find more factual and objective is the ________.
a. rating scale
b. Likert scale
c. performance checklist
d. checklist ____

42. Which grading method provides for a higher frequency of similar ratings on identical criteria among educators or raters?
a. rating scale
b. Likert scale
c. performance checklist
d. checklist ____

43. The method of grading that incorporates scoring of more than one area of learner assessment is known as ________.
a. point grading
b. multiple-category grading
c. performance grading
d. checklist grading ____

44. The method of grading that assigns specific weights to each criterion, allowing the educator to place emphasis on the more important tasks to be completed, is called ________.
a. point grading
b. multiple-category grading
c. performance grading
d. checklist grading ____

45. Testing, both written and practical, is an effective form of measuring and ________ student achievement.
a. estimating
b. evaluating
c. calculating
d. lowering ____

46. Master educators will incorporate a variety of testing and evaluation methods into the training to ensure that all learners reach the desired degree of ________.
a. competency
b. sufficiency
c. adequacy
d. efficiency ____

11 Teaching to Diverse Learning Styles

1. Adult learners tend to be more ________ oriented than other learners.
   a. grades
   b. skills
   c. goal
   d. theory
   _____

2. Adult learners recognize the relevance and need for ________ to make a difference in their careers.
   a. learning
   b. socializing
   c. interacting
   d. direction
   _____

3. One characteristic that researchers and psychologists have identified as common among all adult learners is that of ________.
   a. low motivation
   b. no opinions
   c. unestablished habits
   d. past experience
   _____

4. Because adult learners come to the classroom with behavior patterns contrary to what you are presenting, they may be less ________ than other learners.
   a. flexible
   b. eager
   c. rigid
   d. interested
   _____

5. Adult learners often arrive with established opinions about what is being taught. They need to understand that their ideas and opinions may be ________.
   a. insignificant
   b. outdated
   c. valuable
   d. unnecessary
   _____

6. Adult learners tend to ________ with information or knowledge they already have.
   a. create new theories
   b. make connections
   c. offer arguments
   d. make disassociations
   _____

7. Adult learners are not willing to simply sit in a classroom and receive information ________.
   a. actively
   b. clearly
   c. enthusiastically
   d. passively ____

8. Master educators will challenge adult learners to think and incite learners' ________ to what is occurring in the classroom.
   a. passivity
   b. peacefulness
   c. reaction
   d. opposition ____

9. ________ means to gain knowledge, understanding, and skills by study, instruction, or experience.
   a. Training
   b. Learning
   c. Desiring
   d. Participating ____

10. 4MAT is a natural cycle of learning because it begins with and returns to the ________ and contains all the elements of learning.
    a. classroom
    b. educator
    c. learner
    d. theory ____

11. When educators understand the elements of learning and use the 4MAT cycle to teach, they improve the ________ of their students.
    a. manageability
    b. attitude
    c. emotions
    d. learning ____

12. As children we absorb, examine, experiment, feel, puzzle, attempt, and learn because we are not yet contaminated by fear of ________ or anxious about grades.
    a. failure
    b. success
    c. educators
    d. peers ____

13. The kinds of minds that people come to own are profoundly influenced by the kinds of ________ they have in the course of their lives.
    a. jobs
    b. experiences
    c. attitudes
    d. situations ____

14. A major element in how people learn is ________, how they take in experiences they have.
    a. perceiving
    b. processing
    c. filtering
    d. adapting ____

15. A major element in how people learn is ________, how people react, confront, and resolve what happens to them.
 a. perceiving c. filtering
 b. processing d. adapting ____

16. Learners perceive in two ways: they feel their experiences and they ________ their experiences.
 a. live c. become
 b. act d. think ____

17. When learners encounter something new that intrigues them, they literally go into it feeling and grasping the experience and becoming ________ in it.
 a. fixed c. etched
 b. embedded d. enabled ____

18. As learners reflect on their new experiences, they move into ________ them.
 a. reacting to c. thinking about
 b. acting on d. resolving ____

19. Learners begin with experience at the 12 o'clock position and move to the 6 o'clock position to order and anchor that experience by ________ it.
 a. conceptualizing c. personifying
 b. visualizing d. classifying ____

20. Learners who favor the feeling dimension of learning need to understand the beauty and __________ of thinking.
 a. intellect c. formlessness
 b. aura d. order ____

21. Conceptual thought demands ________ of thinking and feeling.
 a. inclusion c. coupling
 b. separation d. joining ____

22. In addition to perceiving, taking things in, people must do something with the things they are ________ if they are to truly learn them.
 a. experiencing c. conceptualizing
 b. learning d. perceiving ____

23. Adult learners process learning in two ways: they reflect on their experience and they ________ that reflection.
    a. carry on
    b. give up
    c. act on
    d. hold back ______

24. To combine perceiving (taking things in) with processing (doing something with those things) creates a natural ________.
    a. training method
    b. learning activity
    c. learning cycle
    d. relating process ______

25. Learning begins with individuals, their connections to their ________, and it ends when they adapt their use of it in their life.
    a. family
    b. coworkers
    c. experience
    d. classroom ______

26. People who linger in the feeling and watching 12 o'clock to 3 o'clock position of the learning cycle are called ________.
    a. type four learners
    b. type three learners
    c. type two learners
    d. type one learners ______

27. People who linger in thinking and doing 6 o'clock to 9 o'clock position of the learning cycle are called ________.
    a. type four learners
    b. type three learner
    c. type two learners
    d. type one learners ______

28. People who linger in the watching and thinking 3 o'clock to 6 o'clock position of the learning cycle are called ________.
    a. type four learners
    b. type three learners
    c. type two learners
    d. type one learners ______

29. People who linger in the doing and feeling 9 o'clock to 12 o'clock position of the learning cycle are called ________.
    a. type four learners
    b. type three learners
    c. type two learners
    d. type one learners ______

30. Type two and type three learners trust their intellect more than they do their ________.
    a. feelings
    b. skills
    c. abilities
    d. knowledge ______

31. Type one and type four learners trust their feelings more than their ________ .
    a. emotions
    b. intellect
    c. attitudes
    d. misgivings ______

32. Another name for type four learners is ________ learners.
    a. imaginative
    b. analytic
    c. common sense
    d. dynamic _____

33. Another name for type two learners is ________ learners.
    a. imaginative
    b. analytic
    c. common sense
    d. dynamic _____

34. Another name for type three learners is ________ learners.
    a. imaginative
    b. analytic
    c. common sense
    d. dynamic _____

35. Another name for type one learners is ________ learners.
    a. imaginative
    b. analytic
    c. common sense
    d. dynamic _____

36. Imaginative learners perceive information ________ and process it reflectively.
    a. abstractly
    b. concretely
    c. directly
    d. actively _____

37. Analytic learners perceive information abstractly and process it ________.
    a. concretely
    b. directly
    c. actively
    d. reflectively _____

38. Common sense learners perceive information ________ and process it actively.
    a. abstractly
    b. concretely
    c. directly
    d. actively _____

39. Dynamic learners perceive information concretely and process it ________.
    a. abstractly
    b. concretely
    c. passively
    d. actively _____

40. Educators who organize group work and discussions and encourage honest feedback about feelings are ________ learners.
    a. type one
    b. type two
    c. type three
    d. type four _____

41. Learners who love harmony and work diligently to bring it to the lives of the people around them, both personally and professionally, are ________ learners.
a. type one
b. type two
c. type three
d. type four
_____

42. Learners who are very enthusiastic about newness and relish change are ________ learners.
a. type one
b. type two
c. type three
d. type four
_____

43. Learners who are down-to-earth problem-solvers who resent being given the answers are ________ learners.
a. type one
b. type two
c. type three
d. type four
_____

44. Educators who engage in and encourage experiential learning are ________ learners.
a. type one
b. type two
c. type three
d. type four
_____

45. Educators who believe curricula should further understanding of significant information and should be presented systematically are ________ learners.
a. type one
b. type two
c. type three
d. type four
_____

46. Educators who believe curricula should be geared to competencies and economic usefulness are ________ learners.
a. type one
b. type two
c. type three
d. type four
_____

47. The challenge for ________ learners is to act more quickly, move to closure, get the job done even while understanding the need to give people space to process at their own rate.
a. type one
b. type two
c. type three
d. type four
_____

48. The challenge for ________ learners is to develop structure, go deeper, and stay focused, even while understanding the need to cover a lot of territory to break boundaries.
a. type one
b. type two
c. type three
d. type four
_____

49. The challenge for ________ learners is to listen to people, to honor the time people need to discover things for themselves, while understanding the need to get the job done.
a. type one c. type three
b. type two d. type four ____

50. The challenge for ________ learners is to open themselves to the ambiguity of the creative place, even while they understand the need for precision and the "right" data.
a. type one c. type three
b. type two d. type four ____

51. The learners who asks, "*How* does this work? *How* will this streamline tasks? *How* will this be life-useful?" is the ________ learner.
a. type one c. type three
b. type two d. type four ____

52. The learner who asks, "*Why* is this of value personally? *Why* does it need to be connected?" is the ________ learner.
a. type one c. type three
b. type two d. type four ____

53. The learner who asks, "*What* is out there to be known? *What* do the experts know about this? *What* is the nature of the knowledge being pursued here?" is the ________ learner.
a. type one c. type three
b. type two d. type four ____

54. The learner who asks, "*What if* I use this technique this way? *What if* I can create this new concept and possibly change the world?" is the ________ learner.
a. type one c. type three
b. type two d. type four ____

55. For ________ learners, the learning climate is active, doing, trying ideas, seeing from different angles, finding personal uses for the learning, and tinkering with it.
a. type one c. type three
b. type two d. type four ____

56. The learning climate needs to be easy, open, and nurturing for ________ learners.
a. type one c. type three
b. type two d. type four ____

57. The learning climate is dynamic, open-ended, renewing, challenging, boundary breaking, and adapting the learning into something unique for _______ learners.
    a. type one
    b. type two
    c. type three
    d. type four _____

58. For _______ learners the learning climate is receiving, being briefed, writing things down, thoughtfulness, pondering, thinking out loud, and being present to content.
    a. type one
    b. type two
    c. type three
    d. type four _____

59. To reflect and do in equal measure, honoring both, gives our lives the gracefulness of continuous _______.
    a. learning
    b. practice
    c. involvement
    d. connection _____

12 Powerful Teaching and Learning Methods

1. Until graduation the educator will _______ the learner through the teaching and learning process.
   a. direct
   b. lead
   c. accompany
   d. steer _____

2. Teaching is the art of imparting knowledge or _______ by precept, example, or experience.
   a. informing
   b. directing
   c. steering
   d. instructing _____

3. Learning is a modification of a behavioral tendency that occurs due to gaining _______ or understanding through instruction, study, or experience.
   a. knowledge
   b. kindness
   c. praise
   d. esteem _____

4. The manner in which an educator uses available material and resources to achieve desired educational objectives and facilitate learning for all students is known as _______.
   a. teaching idea
   b. teaching method
   c. teaching style
   d. teaching goal _____

5. _______ has its place in our classrooms but is highly effective only with certain types of learners.
   a. Lecture
   b. Demonstration
   c. Question and answer
   d. Testing _____

6. Which teaching method is used to bring the lesson presentation to life?
   a. lecture
   b. demonstration
   c. workbook
   d. testing _____

7. Demonstrations are highly effective in illustrating a/an ________ or clarifying a principle.
   a. theoretical idea
   b. personal philosophy
   c. manipulative procedure
   d. actual theory _____

8. Preparation for a demonstration is essential in that it includes preparing the students for the lesson and motivating them to observe, listen, and ________.
   a. learn
   b. act
   c. talk
   d. study _____

9. When demonstrating, the master educator will avoid ________ and show and explain a single fundamental procedure completely by going through a step-by-step process.
   a. discussions
   b. questions
   c. distractions
   d. discipline _____

10. When demonstrating, the master educator will watch for ________ clues from students that indicate how they are responding to the demonstration and take appropriate action.
    a. nonverbal
    b. vocal
    c. verbal
    d. audible _____

11. Another term for the actual practice or application by students is ________.
    a. student demonstration
    b. instructor application
    c. return demonstration
    d. educator instruction _____

12. Student ________ should occur as soon after the demonstration as possible.
    a. lecturing
    b. theory
    c. study
    d. practice _____

13. Master educators supervise students' practice of a skill and evaluate their performance according to the school's grading policy and predetermined performance ________.
    a. goals
    b. probabilities
    c. criteria
    d. estimates _____

14. Master educators will give ________ and assistance to students participating in the practice session to ensure their work achieves the standards required.
    a. output
    b. feedback
    c. opinions
    d. authority _____

15. In the group discussion and discovery method of learning, learners work in a group environment and share their opinions, judgments, and ________.
    a. mistakes
    b. misunderstandings
    c. failures
    d. perceptions ____

16. Group discussion and discovery is often led by the educator, who provides information and then questions the group in a way that ________ their arrival at the correct answer.
    a. facilitates
    b. diminishes
    c. confuses
    d. curtails ____

17. Group discussion and discovery is extremely advantageous because it requires a high degree of learner ________, which is highly motivating for adult learners.
    a. independence
    b. autonomy
    c. participation
    d. reflection ____

18. The purpose of role-playing in education is to help learners understand the views and feelings of other people with respect to a wide range of ________ issues.
    a. political and social
    b. personal and social
    c. social and physical
    d. social and mental ____

19. In role-playing, the entire class is involved either as a role-player or as an observer who is ________ the enactment and taking notes for later discussion.
    a. conducting
    b. analyzing
    c. directing
    d. leading ____

20. ________ role-playing requires the learner to play the part of a particular job or station rather than a specific individual.
    a. Position
    b. Person
    c. Character
    d. Personality ____

21. An important hint for making role-playing more effective is to use ________ whenever possible.
    a. reluctant students
    b. forced learners
    c. volunteers only
    d. intimidated students ____

22. In ________ role-playing, the learner plays the part of a specific person and acts as that person would in the given situation.
    a. position
    b. scenario
    c. character
    d. situation ____

23. ________ is the process of transferring key elements, points, or steps in a lesson into visual images that are then hand-sketched into the squares of a matrix.
a. Transfer drawing
b. Mind mapping
c. Transfer sketching
d. Window paning ____

24. Research indicates that people can retain in their short-term memory an average of ________ bits of information, with a variation of two on the plus or minus side.
a. five
b. seven
c. eight
d. nine ____

25. Field trips or excursions into the workplace provide students with an opportunity for ________.
a. active learning
b. inactive learning
c. reflective thinking
d. introverted behavior ____

26. In a cooperative effort between the educator and the learners, a determination is made prior to a field trip as to what ________ are to be achieved during the trip.
a. activities
b. ideas
c. conversations
d. objectives ____

27. On return from a field trip there should be an organized review of the event and a/an ________ of the students' observations.
a. written report
b. in-depth discussion
c. quiet reflection
d. classroom reenactment ____

28. Guest speakers can be extremely motivating and can provide important information on related topics on which the educator may have ________.
a. limited knowledge
b. excessive expertise
c. overt abilities
d. achieved excellence ____

29. Master educators recognize that use of a guest speaker does not reduce or eliminate their responsibility to ________.
a. take a break
b. attend and participate
c. give the lecture
d. make telephone calls ____

30. A preliminary meeting with a guest speaker is recommended to set a time frame for the presentation and to set forth any parameters including the ________ of the presentation.
a. introduction
b. humor
c. script
d. objectives ____

31. ________ creates a free-flowing outline of material and information in which the student can organize an entire project or topic in a matter of minutes.
   a. Window paning
   b. Mind mapping
   c. Note taking
   d. Chapter outlining ____

32. In a career training environment where learners have diverse backgrounds and learning styles, one-on-one instruction such as ________ can increase learning results.
   a. group discussion
   b. role-playing
   c. peer coaching
   d. case studies ____

33. Through the use of ________, learners can apply the underlying theories of a subject and integrate them with practice and action.
   a. workbooks
   b. essays
   c. reading
   d. projects ____

34. Master educators will take care to use workbook activity as a complement to, not a substitute for, ________.
   a. field trips
   b. instruction
   c. window paning
   d. visualization ____

35. The use of ________ handouts aids the learners because they do not have to write down everything being covered.
   a. colored ink
   b. totally blank
   c. partially complete
   d. handmade ____

36. The use of ________ as a teaching method is effective because it provides detailed descriptions of realistic problem situations that require resolution.
   a. role-playing
   b. case studies
   c. group discussions
   d. class contests ____

37. A ________ will link the learner's experience with the skill or information that is being conveyed in the lesson.
   a. thought connector
   b. language link
   c. mind map
   d. concept connector ____

38. ________ is the process by which the mind translates the content of a lesson into visual imagery.
   a. Self-suggestion
   b. Imagination
   c. Translation
   d. Visualization ____

39. Stories, brief anecdotes, or ________ may be used in the classroom to describe or explain a specific point or process even though they will not always prove it.
    a. lectures c. activities
    b. demonstrations d. testimonials _____

40. The technique of using a word or phrase association, songs, or any other method to trigger in the memory key terms or information contained in a lesson is ________.
    a. mnemonics c. memorization
    b. phonics d. megamemory _____

41. A brief activity that may take only 1 to 3 minutes and provides both mental and physical breaks for the learners is known as a/an ________.
    a. exercise c. project
    b. energizer d. discussion _____

42. By using ________ in the classroom, the educator allows learners to translate the content of the lesson into a personage.
    a. personifications c. characterizations
    b. identifications d. transformations _____

43. A/An ________ is an operation or procedure carried out under controlled conditions to discover an unknown effect or result or to illustrate a known effect or law.
    a. exercise c. experiment
    b. project d. demonstration _____

44. When learners are ________, they feel good and their minds are open to new experiences and ideas.
    a. laughing c. glowering
    b. frowning d. complaining _____

45. The use of humor in the classroom should be timely and ________, not planned in advance.
    a. scheduled c. professional
    b. practiced d. natural _____

46. Master educators will observe and monitor group activity but will not ________ group discussions even when the group appears to be at a roadblock.
    a. assist c. facilitate
    b. aid d. take over _____

47. Learners will gain tremendous _______ through the group exploration, struggling, and discovery process.
    a. discomfort
    b. self-confidence
    c. self-control
    d. dissatisfaction _____

48. A true master educator will never limit his _______ and will work to develop his own creativity to bring more variety, enthusiasm, and energy into the classroom.
    a. predictability
    b. satisfaction
    c. complacency
    d. imagination _____

13 Achieving Learner Results

1. The provisions of the Americans with Disabilities Act of 1990 (ADA) prohibit ________ against people with disabilities.
   a. recrimination
   b. indemnification
   c. discrimination
   d. edification _____

2. Disabled students desiring to enroll in a post-secondary institution must provide ________ of their disability and formally request accommodations and access to classes.
   a. history
   b. documentation
   c. photographs
   d. narratives _____

3. The accommodation plan offered by an institution to a disabled learner describes the steps the school can reasonably take to accommodate the individual's ________.
   a. special interests
   b. special program
   c. ordinary needs
   d. special needs _____

4. If a disabled learner does not report a special need to the school, the school is not ________ by law to provide specific accommodations.
   a. exempt
   b. excusable
   c. responsible
   d. unfettered _____

5. Qualified interpreters, listening devices, note taker, and written materials for individuals with hearing impairments are known as ________.
   a. auxiliary aids and services
   b. special helps and services
   c. special aids and needs
   d. auxiliary impediments and services _____

6. Qualified readers, taped texts, and Braille or large-print materials for individuals with vision impairments are known as ________.
   a. auxiliary aids and services
   b. special helps and services
   c. special aids and needs
   d. auxiliary impediments and services
   _____

7. A specific learning disability that hinders the learning of literacy or reading skills is known as ________.
   a. hyperactivity
   b. dyslexia
   c. diabetes
   d. addiction
   _____

8. If an educator observes the symptoms of dyslexia, the learner should be ________.
   a. referred to a diagnostic specialist
   b. terminated from course enrollment
   c. placed in a separate classroom
   d. given extra homework daily
   _____

9. Some dyslexic learners experience difficulty in carrying out ________ instructions in sequence.
   a. confusing
   b. two
   c. three
   d. six
   _____

10. Educators will find that many dyslexic learners have a good visual eye; are imaginative, skillful with their hands, and ________; and often excel at individual sports.
    a. impractical
    b. idealistic
    c. unrealistic
    d. practical
    _____

11. One teaching tip for educators of dyslexic learners is to use highly focused teaching, whenever possible, in groups of ________ students.
    a. 2 to 3
    b. 4 to 5
    c. 5 to 7
    d. 7 to 10
    _____

12. One teaching tip for educators of dyslexic learners is to use structured, ________ methods for teaching and have students use similar methods for practicing and learning.
    a. singular
    b. multisensory
    c. favorite
    d. listening
    _____

13. One teaching tip for educators of dyslexic learners is to ________; remember their difficulty in trying to achieve success; and reading and writing.
    a. ignore their attempts
    b. reprimand their daydreaming
    c. praise their efforts
    d. stay on track ____

14. One behavior to avoid when teaching dyslexic learners is making them ________ in class if they do not wish to do so.
    a. take notes
    b. read aloud
    c. do projects
    d. give handouts ____

15. One thought an educator should remember about dyslexic learners is that they may omit words or write words ________.
    a. upside down
    b. in another language
    c. twice
    d. backward ____

16. ADD is a learning disability also known as ________.
    a. attention daydreaming disorder
    b. actual deficit disorder
    c. attention definite disorder
    d. attention deficit disorder ____

17. ADD is defined as "a chronic neurological dysfunction with the ________ system and is not related to gender, level of intelligence, or cultural environment."
    a. central nervous
    b. lymphatic
    c. skeletal
    d. muscular ____

18. Statistically, ________ % of school-age children are diagnosed with ADD.
    a. 1 to 3
    b. 3 to 5
    c. 3 to 8
    d. 5 to 9 ____

19. Of those school-age children diagnosed with ADD, ________ are boys compared to 1 girl.
    a. 2 to 3
    b. 3 to 4
    c. 4 to 5
    d. 5 to 6 ____

20. Symptoms of ADD include inattention, ________, impulsiveness, social ineptness, inconsistency and continuity, and behavior problems in more than one environment.
    a. passivity
    b. inactivity
    c. hyperactivity
    d. lethargy ____

21. ________ by others is critical to the success of the ADD learner.
   a. Assistance
   b. Criticism
   c. Rejection
   d. Acceptance _____

22. Building ________ and setting goals are essential for ADD learners to attain optimal living.
   a. personal objectives
   b. self-esteem
   c. self-perception
   d. personal desire _____

23. One strategy for teaching ADD learners is to seat them in a ________ area with few or no distractions especially when they need to study or take tests.
   a. noisy
   b. active
   c. busy
   d. quiet _____

24. One strategy for teaching ADD learners is to prepare them in advance for changes in ________.
   a. methods
   b. techniques
   c. routine
   d. spontaneity _____

25. One strategy for teaching ADD learners is to allow sufficient time for them to thoughtfully consider questions and ________.
   a. prepare answers
   b. pose problems
   c. consider alternatives
   d. change the subject _____

26. One strategy for teaching ADD learners is to give ________ prior to tests.
   a. additional homework
   b. special projects
   c. practice quizzes
   d. written assignments _____

27. One strategy for teaching ADD learners is to use ________ tests or handouts.
   a. handwritten
   b. typewritten
   c. complicated
   d. lengthy _____

28. Master educators must learn to be ________ and accept behavior or performance from ADD learners that may not meet the standards they have established for other learners.
   a. rigid
   b. constrained
   c. formal
   d. flexible _____

29. ADD learners can achieve the goal of independence only when they are given appropriate supports, have mastered time management and planning, and feel ________.
   a. in control and comfortable
   b. threatened and fearful
   c. uncomfortable and flexible
   d. stressed and comfortable _____

30. The American workforce is composed of 10% alcoholics, 10% problem drinkers, 4% drug users, and _____% mentally disturbed people.
   a. 10
   b. 15
   c. 20
   d. 25 _____

31. Some of the symptoms of chronic negative behaviors are inattentiveness, memory lapses, ________, improper diet, lack of motivation and interest, and poor self-esteem.
   a. high self-confidence
   b. poor attendance
   c. positive attitude
   d. clear thinking _____

32. Master educators should not attempt to label learners with disabilities or even ________ chronic behavioral problems.
   a. describe
   b. identify
   c. diagnose
   d. refer _____

33. If a master educator observes chronic behavior indicative of alcoholism, drug abuse, or mental disturbance, she should refer the learner to ________.
   a. a school administrator
   b. a professional source
   c. a health school
   d. legal counsel _____

34. One of the most common barriers to learning that students may bring with them to the classroom is ________.
   a. contentment
   b. excitement
   c. tranquility
   d. anxiety _____

35. One step an educator can take to help relieve learner apprehension is to be ________.
   a. empathic
   b. firm
   c. rigid
   d. regimented _____

36. One step an educator can take to help relieve learner apprehension is to treat each learner as ________.
   a. a student
   b. an ally
   c. an individual
   d. if ordinary _____

37. A master educator will encourage learners who are fearful to build their ________.
   a. goals
   b. self-confidence
   c. self-realization
   d. portfolio _____

38. With fearful learners, limit the ________ of learning activities.
   a. use
   b. number
   c. evaluation
   d. repetition _____

39. Master educators will avoid being in ________ with learners, especially those who are apprehensive.
   a. harmony
   b. conformity
   c. accord
   d. competition _____

40. One barrier to learning for adult learners that master educators must learn to deal with in the classroom is learner ________.
   a. recall
   b. receptiveness
   c. knowledge
   d. willingness _____

41. ________ are any type of hint or signal that indicates the nature of something to be remembered.
   a. Hand gestures
   b. Memory cues
   c. Word games
   d. Memory lapses _____

42. Master educators will develop a portfolio of memory cues that can be used in the ________ process.
   a. practical
   b. development
   c. educational
   d. informational _____

43. An accommodation plan for disabled students might address environment, lesson presentation, assignments, testing, organizational planning, and educator ________.
   a. skills and abilities
   b. knowledge and skills
   c. behaviors and attitudes
   d. speech and deportment _____

44. Master educators will provide opportunities for ________ and eliminate, whenever possible, the requirement for learners to respond immediately.
   a. inattention
   b. self-pacing
   c. timing
   d. pressure _____

45. A serious barrier to learning occurs when there is a lack of ________.
   a. learner motivation
   b. learner lethargy
   c. learner apathy
   d. learner disinterest _____

46. Some of the greatest barriers to learning may be created by the _______ of the educator.
a. skills and abilities
b. knowledge and skills
c. behaviors and attitudes
d. speech and deportment _____

47. One barrier to learning caused by the educator is failure to establish strong _______ with the learners.
a. personal relationships
b. personal contact
c. professional rules
d. classroom guidelines _____

48. One barrier to learning caused by the educator is the failure to allow learners the opportunity to interact with others and experience _______.
a. individual growth
b. individual counseling
c. peer support
d. peer criticism _____

49. You will remain powerless as an educator if you never develop the skills required to _______ your knowledge.
a. withhold
b. reserve
c. preserve
d. communicate _____

50. To communicate clearly is to transmit information, thought, or feeling so that it is satisfactorily received and _______.
a. heard
b. written
c. understood
d. explained _____

51. _______ communication can be added to spoken communication to change or enhance the meaning.
a. Written
b. Nonverbal
c. Oral
d. Detailed _____

52. _______ is the receiver's way of acknowledging the message or information.
a. Feedback
b. Output
c. Input
d. Return _____

53. The packaging and controlling of a message is called _______.
a. decoding
b. encoding
c. procoding
d. precoding _____

54. Interpreting the message and providing feedback to the message is called _______.
a. decoding
b. encoding
c. procoding
d. precoding _____

55. In the first step in the communication cycle, the educator packages information or skills by _______ it into words, symbols, signs, or behavior that the learner can understand.
a. decoding
b. encoding
c. procoding
d. precoding _____

56. In the second step in the communication cycle, the learner opens the package by _______ the skills or information by interpreting the educator's words, symbols, or behavior.
a. decoding
b. encoding
c. procoding
d. precoding _____

57. In the third step in the communication cycle, the learner packages a response by _______ her understanding of the message into a new message that is sent back to the educator.
a. decoding
b. encoding
c. procoding
d. precoding _____

58. In the fourth step of the communication cycle, the educator _______ the response to determine whether the skills or information were understood by the learner.
a. decodes
b. encodes
c. procodes
d. precodes _____

59. An effective way to communicate that is useful when dealing with conflict situations or in student counseling is known as _______.
a. passive listening
b. active listening
c. passive speech
d. active speech _____

60. The art of listening is not easy and requires an open mind and appreciation of the _______ your peers and your learners have to make.
a. limitations
b. discountenance
c. contributions
d. acknowledgments _____

61. One effective study habit is to take _______ and be responsible for your learning because no one can make you learn.
a. credit
b. authority
c. breaks
d. charge _____

62. It has been said that 80% of success is _______.
a. showing up
b. playing hard
c. looking ahead
d. working late _____

63. One effective study habit is to construct a comprehensive ________ from general long-term to short-term daily.
   a. plan
   b. schedule
   c. thought
   d. outline
   _____

64. One effective study habit is to have a regular place for studying that is free of ________ and other people.
   a. dust
   b. fresh air
   c. distractions
   d. good lighting
   _____

65. Adopting a mascot that you use each time you study will aid in your ________.
   a. ability
   b. concentration
   c. knowledge
   d. practice
   _____

66. An effective technique to use when you are studying and your mind begins to wander or you begin to daydream is to ________.
   a. stand up and look away
   b. get up and study later
   c. refocus and read chapter again
   d. force yourself to concentrate
   _____

67. Make sure not to start a lengthy project or go back to any former ________ just before your scheduled study time.
   a. review chapters
   b. study locations
   c. unfinished tasks
   d. unfinished assignment
   _____

68. By dividing study work into "mini" assignments, you will feel a sense of ________ as you complete each one and that will make continued study easier.
   a. regret
   b. accomplishment
   c. challenge
   d. irritation
   _____

69. One strategy for studying effectively is to begin with the ________ part first.
   a. easy
   b. quick
   c. difficult
   d. irrelevant
   _____

70. Learners can take action in the face of their study fears and avoid barriers to learning by also avoiding ________ in education.
   a. school attendance
   b. doing homework
   c. learner relationships
   d. failure behaviors
   _____

71. For learning to occur, learners must follow a balanced diet, get appropriate weekly exercise, and remain free of ________.
a. daily fresh air
b. a positive attitude
c. drugs and alcohol
d. slow, rhythmic breathing ______

14 Professional Performance Evaluation

1. Master educators recognize that to meet the challenges presented by their diverse learners, they must engage in constant professional _______ and self-improvement.
   a. praise
   b. assessment
   c. appeasement
   d. justification _____

2. Professional improvement will have greater impact and be longer lasting when the educator recognizes the need for improved performance and defines a _______ to achieve it.
   a. personal short-term goal
   b. professional action approach
   c. professional development plan
   d. method and approach _____

3. By adopting a/an _______ to self-improvement and following self-improvement strategies, educators inspire learners to become highly skilled, competent professionals.
   a. positive attitude
   b. lethargic approach
   c. apathetic attitude
   d. easygoing approach _____

4. A professional performance evaluation is an appraisal of performance based on _______.
   a. interest
   b. desires
   c. recruitments
   d. expectations _____

5. Nine areas of performance usually reviewed are production, accuracy, independent action, methods, problem-solving, interpersonal skills, work habits, and _______.
   a. cost consciousness and reading skill
   b. cost consciousness and self-motivation
   c. self-motivation and reading skill
   d. self-motivation and hair color _____

6. One criterion for evaluating an educator's level of production might be that she goes above and beyond normal production requirements and assumes ________ when needed.
   a. extra duties
   b. appropriate attitudes
   c. cost-saving technique
   d. written assignments ____

7. When evaluating an educator's thoroughness and accuracy, one criterion might be that she verifies ________ information or procedures.
   a. daily
   b. regular
   c. questionable
   d. clear ____

8. In determining an educator's ability to work independently, one criterion might be that he exercises ________ in starting and following through on assigned work.
   a. organization
   b. initiative
   c. priorities
   d. cooperation ____

9. One area of work methods that might be evaluated for an educator is whether she initiates prompt ________ when goals are not met.
   a. organized tasks
   b. disciplinary action
   c. corrective actions
   d. time wasters ____

10. One evaluation criterion for educators might be whether they evaluate all possible ________ before taking action.
    a. problems
    b. causes
    c. outcomes
    d. challenges ____

11. One evaluation criterion for educators might be whether they work ________ with coworkers, students, clients, and management.
    a. independently
    b. cooperatively
    c. intensely
    d. critically ____

12. One evaluation criterion for educators might be whether they keep a professional distance from students and never ________ them.
    a. fraternize with
    b. plan work for
    c. give assistance to
    d. provide counseling for ____

13. Educators might be evaluated by their superiors on their dependable, regular ________.
    a. attitude
    b. emotions
    c. delivery
    d. attendance ____

14. When evaluating cost consciousness, an educator might be evaluated in her observation of energy-saving measures with respect to products, ________, and laundry.
    a. towel
    b. services
    c. clients
    d. utilities ____

15. One criterion on which an educator might be evaluated is whether he sustains a high level of ________ and enthusiasm.
    a. apathy
    b. interest
    c. unwillingness
    d. lethargy ____

16. Sources from which the educator can obtain assessment of personal performance include supervisors, students, peers, ________, employers of graduates, and self.
    a. spouses
    b. children
    c. graduates
    d. parents ____

17. Supervisors are responsible for training educators in the proper procedures and expected ________ as well as providing assistance, coaching, or direction to educators.
    a. attitudes
    b. emotions
    c. behaviors
    d. philosophies ____

18. Fellow educators can provide another educator with a/an ________, fresh perspective of how she is doing on the job.
    a. intimidating
    b. critical
    c. fearful
    d. nonthreatening ____

19. Learners can give educators valuable feedback regarding the educational methods used, the ________ established with the learners, the use of visual aids, and much more.
    a. rules
    b. regulations
    c. relationships
    d. schedules ____

20. The achievements of graduates on the job and the competitiveness of their ________ may directly or indirectly relate to the educator's ability and performance.
    a. entry-level skills
    b. professional attitudes
    c. retail sales skills
    d. long-term skills ____

21. In your quest to become a master educator, you must recognize that ________ is never attained in any career pursuit.
    a. simple mediocrity
    b. average performance
    c. unsatisfactory performance
    d. absolute perfection ____

22. Once feedback regarding the educator's performance has been received from the various sources, the educator can use that feedback to create a ________.
a. personal short-term goal
b. professional action approach
c. professional development plan
d. method and approach ____

23. In developing a plan for improvement of performance, the educator should establish long-term goals that are supported by ________ that can be measured.
a. short-term objectives
b. long-term objectives
c. task assignments
d. dreams and desires ____

24. As part of the formal plan for improvement, the educator should outline the ________ that will be required to achieve any established objectives.
a. dreams and desires
b. tasks and hopes
c. satisfactory performance
d. strategies or activities ____

25. The first step in creating a professional development plan for improvement would be to simply state the ________.
a. problem area or concerns
b. purpose of the plan
c. strategies and solutions
d. overview of the plan ____

26. In the second step of creating a professional development plan for improvement, the educator will briefly identify one or two ________ for improved performance or behavior.
a. long-term goals
b. short-term objectives
c. expected learner outcomes
d. strategies and activities ____

27. In the third step of creating a professional development plan for improvement, the educator will list specific ________ that are measurable.
a. long-term goals
b. short-term objectives
c. expected learner outcomes
d. strategies and activities ____

28. In the fourth step of creating a professional development plan for improvement, the educator will list ________.
a. long-term goals
b. short-term objectives
c. expected learner outcomes
d. strategies and activities ____

29. In the fifth step of creating a professional development, the educator identifies specific ________ that should result in the achievement of stated objectives.
a. long-term goals
b. short-term objectives
c. expected learner outcomes
d. strategies and activities ____

30. In the sixth step in the creation of a professional development plan for improvement, the educator will ________.
    a. evaluate its effectiveness
    b. write down the results
    c. report results to supervisor
    d. determine results orally _____

31. The final step in the use of a professional development plan for improvement calls for ________.
    a. peer feedback
    b. learner feedback
    c. personal feedback
    d. supervisory feedback _____

32. A sure step toward the attainment and maintenance of master educator status is to constantly further one's ________.
    a. position
    b. politics
    c. education
    d. visibility _____

33. Master educators avail themselves of every opportunity for professional development and do not consider ________ standards of performance or education acceptable.
    a. minimum
    b. maximum
    c. superior
    d. unsurpassed _____

15 Preparing for Licensure and Employment

1. Factors affecting how learners do on tests include physical and psychological well-being, time management, and skills in reading, note taking, test-taking, and ________.
   a. memory and writing
   b. conversation and writing
   c. discussion and outlining
   d. role-playing and writing ______

2. The first and foremost way for any learner to do well on any test is to be thoroughly familiar with ________.
   a. test-taking strategies
   b. course content
   c. the educator's style
   d. course outlines ______

3. Test-taking skills are a must for all learners if the test results are to be ________.
   a. considered
   b. reviewed
   c. valid
   d. irrelevant ______

4. Good students who are not wise in test-taking skills may lose out in competitive situations to ________ students who are weaker or know less.
   a. smarter
   b. older
   c. talented
   d. test-wise ______

5. Test-wise learners are less intimidated by tests and may do better than other students because they have less ________.
   a. test anxiety
   b. test interest
   c. test preparation
   d. study time ______

6. Master educators will ensure that all learners have the opportunity to clearly understand the ________ of the test.
   a. sequence
   b. scheduling
   c. purpose
   d. irrelevance ______

7. Learners should be experienced in using test ________.
   a. score sheets
   b. outlines
   c. questions
   d. materials ____

8. Learners should have experience following ________ similar to those that will be used during the test.
   a. classroom rules
   b. classroom arrangements
   c. test directions
   d. lesson formats ____

9. Learners should be taught the importance of reading each test question ________.
   a. at a glance
   b. carefully
   c. sporadically
   d. inattentively ____

10. Before learners actually take a test, they should begin to get mentally and physically ready by developing a ________.
    a. test attitude
    b. test plan
    c. positive attitude
    d. thorough outline ____

11. One step learners can take to prepare for a test is to follow a healthy diet and get plenty of ________ during the weeks preceding the test.
    a. rest
    b. relaxation
    c. energy
    d. exercise ____

12. Learners should avoid ________ the night before an examination.
    a. eating
    b. sleeping
    c. cramming
    d. reviewing ____

13. One strategy learners can use on the day of the test is to relax and try to ________.
    a. eat a huge meal
    b. slow down physically
    c. sleep later than usual
    d. slow down mentally ____

14. One strategy learners can use on the day of the test is to review the material ________ if possible.
    a. thoroughly
    b. completely
    c. lightly
    d. heavily ____

15. One strategy learners can use on the day of the test is to arrive alert and calm and with the correct ________ attitude.
    a. self-confident
    b. contagious
    c. intellectual
    d. personal ____

16. Before beginning to take the test, learners should ________.
    a. read the entire test
    b. skim the entire test
    c. reread the chapter
    d. mark the first answer ____

17. When taking tests, learners should begin work ________ and mark the answers in the test booklet carefully but quickly.
    a. as soon as possible
    b. after reading the test
    c. at the last minute
    d. before the directions are given ____

18. One time-saving method in test-taking is to answer the ________ questions first.
    a. hardest
    b. longest
    c. shortest
    d. easiest ____

19. When unsure of the answer to a test question, the learner should ________ the question for identification later.
    a. mark
    b. underline
    c. circle
    d. answer ____

20. Learners should answer as many questions as possible first and then return to unanswered questions and ________ the correct answers.
    a. mark only
    b. guess or estimate
    c. identify only
    d. remember only ____

21. Learners should look over the test when they are done to be sure they have answered as many as possible; they should make changes only if there is a/an ________ to do so.
    a. reason
    b. directive
    c. delusion
    d. impulse ____

22. Deductive ________ allows learners to reach a logical conclusion when taking tests by using logical thinking.
    a. speculation
    b. estimation
    c. reasoning
    d. equivocation ____

23. One test-taking strategy is to watch for key words or terms and looking closely for ________ conditions or statements.
    a. qualifying
    b. deficient
    c. unsuitable
    d. efficacious ____

24. One test-taking strategy is to study the stem, which will often provide a/an ________ in deciding the answer.
    a. guess c. estimate
    b. clue d. stab ____

25. When answering a true or false question, learners should watch for ________ words.
    a. deficient c. misspelled
    b. qualifying d. negative ____

26. In true/false questions, ________ statements are more likely to be true because the detail is needed to provide factual data.
    a. short c. long
    b. abbreviated d. simple ____

27. When taking multiple choice tests, read the entire question carefully, including all the ________.
    a. correct options c. distracters
    b. foils d. all of the above ____

28. *All of the above* types of responses in multiple choice questions are likely to be the ________ response.
    a. correct c. only
    b. incorrect d. longest ____

29. In multiple choice questions, when two options are identical, both must be ________.
    a. correct c. considered
    b. incorrect d. selected ____

30. When taking tests that contain matching questions, learners should ________ items from the right-hand list to eliminate choices.
    a. remove c. check off
    b. read d. ignore ____

31. One strategy to follow when taking essay question tests is to ________ before beginning to write your response.
    a. exercise c. practice
    b. rest d. brainstorm ____

32. Master educators should treat each test as a ________ experience for students.
    a. new c. learning
    b. repeat d. horrifying ____

33. Master educators will be positive and ________ with students when discussing the test-taking process.
  a. enthusiastic c. monotonous
  b. reticent d. apathetic ____

34. One of the first steps in the process of securing employment as an educator is to complete the Personal Inventory of ________.
  a. Characteristics and Skills c. Characteristics and Emotions
  b. Skills and Attitudes d. Skills and Abilities ____

35. A ________ is used to summarize your education and work experience and tell potential employers at a glance what your achievements and accomplishments are.
  a. portfolio c. personal history
  b. resumé d. biography ____

36. One basic thing to remember when preparing your professional resumé is to keep it simple and ________ if at all possible.
  a. to one page c. on yellow paper
  b. to two pages d. include all work experience ____

37. Have your resumé printed on good-quality bond paper that is either white, buff, or ________.
  a. yellow c. blue
  b. gray d. light green ____

38. ________ statements in your resumé should always enlarge on your basic duties and responsibilities.
  a. Theoretical c. Accomplishment
  b. Judgment d. Informational ____

39. In writing your resumé, attempt to quantify your accomplishments by adding numbers or ________ whenever possible.
  a. testimonials c. percentages
  b. anecdotes d. analogies ____

40. There is no better time than while you are in school, training to become a master educator, to achieve significant ________ that will impress a potential employer.
  a. quotas c. objectives
  b. goals d. accomplishments ____

41. Your employment ________ is your opportunity to brag about yourself and let your career accomplishments shine.
   a. history
   b. portfolio
   c. performance
   d. biography ____

42. Diplomas, awards, achievements, your resumé, a synopsis of your continuing education, and ________ should all be included in your portfolio.
   a. personal portrait
   b. family photos
   c. letters of reference
   d. personal hobbies ____

43. When looking for a school in which you may wish to teach, a key tip is to locate one that serves the type of ________ you wish to serve.
   a. students and clients
   b. clients and friends
   c. salespeople and clients
   d. students and families ____

44. An indirect method of job hunting is a method called ________.
   a. contacting
   b. targeting
   c. networking
   d. locating ____

45. Whenever possible you should visit and ________ the school before you have an employment interview.
   a. photograph
   b. observe
   c. attend
   d. call ____

46. When you visit an institution before seeking employment there, use a ________ to ensure that you observe all the key areas that might ultimately affect an employment decision.
   a. checklist
   b. visit form
   c. notepad
   d. interview form ____

47. After graduation, having observed the school(s) where you may wish to be employed, you should contact them by sending a resumé and ________ requesting an interview.
   a. gift certificate
   b. cover letter
   c. photograph
   d. checklist ____

48. The resumé should be followed up with ________.
   a. a thank-you note
   b. another letter
   c. a telephone call
   d. a personal visit ____

49. In preparing for an interview, make a list of items typically asked for on an employment application, such as Social Security number, former employers, and _______.

a. personal dietary habits
b. personal hobbies
c. driver's license number
d. clothing size

_____

50. It is recommended that you obtain _______ interview outfit(s).

a. one
b. two
c. three
d. four

_____

51. When selecting an interview outfit, make sure it is comfortable, _______, and a style and color that are flattering to your shape and personality.

a. in good shape
b. dry cleaned
c. in perfect condition
d. well-worn

_____

52. Items you need to take to the employment interview include another resumé, facts and figures regarding your personal information and work history, and your _______.

a. employment portfolio
b. briefcase
c. personal photograph
d. pay stub

_____

53. An important behavior to remember for the employment interview is _______.

a. be prompt and abrupt
b. always be on time
c. fidget and offer a cigarette
d. be reserved

_____

54. An important behavior to remember during the employment interview is to think questions and answers through carefully and not speak for more than _______ minute(s) at a time.

a. 1
b. 2
c. 5
d. 7

_____

55. After employment it is important to access a copy of the school's _______ at the earliest opportunity.

a. clinic price list
b. student body roster
c. inventory sheets
d. operating procedures

_____

56. As an employee various taxes may be withheld from your paycheck, including federal income tax, possible state income tax, worker's compensation, and _______.

a. FICA
b. FUTA
c. SUTA
d. PITA

_____

57. One of the initial steps you should take upon employment as an educator is to become familiar with the school's ________.
    a. catalog
    b. tuition and fees
    c. clinic price list
    d. curriculum _____

58. The more familiar you become with class schedules, course outlines and requirements, grading procedures, and so forth, the less likely you are to ________ early in your employment.
    a. get an early promotion
    b. get a pay raise
    c. make needless mistakes
    d. score bonus points _____

59. As an educator you must remain healthy and ________ if you are to serve your institution well.
    a. overworked
    b. exhausted
    c. energetic
    d. lethargic _____

60. If you should find yourself as a new educator a member of a school team that is rife with petty disagreements and infighting or jealousy, keep ________.
    a. a constant vigil
    b. a positive attitude
    c. a notebook of events
    d. on the winning side _____

Answer Key

Chapter 1

1. b
2. c
3. b
4. c
5. c
6. d
7. b
8. c
9. a
10. d
11. b
12. c
13. a
14. a
15. b
16. c
17. b
18. a
19. b
20. c

Chapter 2

1. a
2. c
3. b
4. d
5. a
6. d
7. c
8. b
9. c
10. b
11. a
12. b
13. d
14. c
15. b
16. b
17. c
18. a
19. b
20. d
21. a
22. c
23. b
24. d
25. a

Chapter 3

1. b
2. a
3. c
4. d
5. c
6. b
7. a
8. d
9. c
10. b
11. c
12. a
13. b
14. c
15. a

Chapter 4

1. b
2. c
3. c
4. b
5. a
6. b
7. c
8. d
9. a
10. b
11. a
12. c
13. c
14. a
15. d
16. b
17. a
18. a
19. d
20. b
21. a
22. c
23. b
24. c
25. b
26. b
27. d
28. c
29. b
30. a
31. b
32. c
33. b
34. c
35. d
36. c
37. a
38. c
39. d
40. b
41. b
42. c
43. a
44. d
45. b
46. c
47. c
48. a
49. b
50. c

Chapter 5

1. b
2. a
3. c
4. a
5. d
6. c
7. d
8. b
9. a
10. c
11. b
12. d
13. c
14. b
15. c
16. a
17. d
18. a
19. a
20. b
21. c
22. d
23. a
24. d
25. d
26. c
27. d
28. a
29. c
30. b
31. b
32. a
33. d
34. a
35. c
36. b
37. c
38. b
39. c
40. a
41. b
42. d
43. b
44. a
45. d
46. c
47. d
48. c
49. b
50. d

Chapter 6

1. b
2. c
3. d
4. c
5. b
6. d
7. c
8. b
9. a
10. b
11. d
12. a
13. c
14. c
15. d
16. c
17. d
18. a
19. b
20. b
21. a
22. b
23. c
24. d
25. a
26. c
27. d
28. b
29. a
30. d
31. b
32. d
33. b
34. a
35. c
36. d
37. c
38. d
39. a
40. d
41. c
42. b
43. a
44. d
45. b
46. c
47. b
48. a
49. b
50. d
51. b
52. a
53. b
54. c
55. d
56. d
57. c
58. b
59. a
60. c
61. d
62. b
63. d
64. c
65. a
66. d
67. b
68. c
69. d
70. c
71. c
72. b

Chapter 7

1. b
2. c
3. a
4. d
5. c
6. c
7. a
8. d
9. c
10. a
11. c
12. a
13. b
14. d
15. c
16. d
17. b
18. d
19. c
20. b
21. c
22. d
23. c
24. a
25. c
26. d
27. a
28. c
29. b
30. a
31. b
32. a
33. d
34. b
35. c
36. b
37. c
38. b
39. a
40. c
41. b
42. c
43. d
44. b
45. b
46. a
47. c
48. a
49. b
50. c

Chapter 8

1. a
2. b
3. c
4. b
5. d
6. c
7. a
8. a
9. c
10. d
11. a
12. b
13. c
14. d
15. c
16. b
17. b
18. c
19. b
20. c
21. c
22. a
23. b
24. c
25. d
26. b
27. b
28. c
29. b
30. a
31. c
32. a
33. b
34. c
35. d

Chapter 9

1. c
2. b
3. d
4. a
5. d
6. c
7. c
8. d
9. b
10. b
11. d
12. c
13. a
14. b
15. c
16. c
17. a
18. b
19. c
20. d
21. a
22. b
23. a
24. d
25. c
26. b
27. a
28. c
29. c
30. d
31. c
32. a
33. a
34. c
35. b
36. b
37. d
38. b
39. b
40. c
41. a
42. c
43. a
44. b
45. c
46. c
47. a
48. d
49. a
50. b
51. a
52. b
53. c
54. b
55. b
56. a
57. c
58. b
59. c
60. a
61. b
62. c
63. a
64. d
65. a
66. d
67. b
68. c
69. a
70. b

Chapter 10

1. c
2. a
3. a
4. b
5. c
6. a
7. d
8. b
9. c
10. b
11. c
12. d
13. a
14. b
15. c
16. a
17. b
18. c
19. b
20. a
21. a
22. d
23. c
24. b
25. a
26. a
27. d
28. c
29. b
30. d
31. a
32. b
33. a
34. b
35. c
36. a
37. c
38. b
39. a
40. d
41. c
42. c
43. b
44. a
45. b
46. a

Chapter 11

1. c
2. a
3. d
4. a
5. c
6. b
7. d
8. c
9. b
10. c
11. d
12. a
13. b
14. a
15. b
16. d
17. b
18. c
19. a
20. d
21. b
22. a
23. c
24. c
25. c
26. d
27. b
28. c
29. a
30. a
31. b
32. d
33. b
34. c
35. a
36. b
37. d
38. a
39. d
40. a
41. a
42. d
43. c
44. d
45. b
46. c
47. a
48. d
49. c
50. b
51. c
52. a
53. b
54. d
55. c
56. a
57. d
58. b
59. a

Chapter 12

1. c
2. d
3. a
4. b
5. a
6. b
7. c
8. a
9. c
10. a
11. c
12. d
13. c
14. b
15. d
16. a
17. c
18. b
19. b
20. a
21. c
22. c
23. d
24. b
25. a
26. d
27. b
28. a
29. b
30. d
31. b
32. c
33. d
34. b
35. c
36. b
37. d
38. d
39. d
40. a
41. b
42. c
43. c
44. a
45. d
46. d
47. b
48. d

Chapter 13

1. c
2. b
3. d
4. c
5. a
6. a
7. b
8. a
9. c
10. d
11. a
12. b
13. c
14. b
15. c
16. d
17. a
18. c
19. b
20. c
21. d
22. b
23. d
24. c
25. a
26. c
27. b
28. d
29. a
30. c
31. b
32. c
33. b
34. d
35. a
36. c
37. b
38. c
39. d
40. a
41. b
42. c
43. c
44. b
45. a
46. c
47. b
48. c
49. d
50. c
51. b
52. a
53. b
54. a
55. b
56. a
57. b
58. a
59. b
60. c
61. d
62. a
63. b
64. c
65. b
66. a
67. c
68. b
69. c
70. d
71. c

Chapter 14

1. b
2. c
3. a
4. d
5. b
6. a
7. c
8. b
9. c
10. c
11. b
12. a
13. d
14. d
15. b
16. c
17. c
18. d
19. c
20. a
21. d
22. c
23. a
24. d
25. a
26. a
27. b
28. c
29. d
30. a
31. d
32. c
33. a

Chapter 15

1. a	16. b	31. d	46. a
2. b	17. a	32. c	47. b
3. c	18. d	33. a	48. c
4. d	19. a	34. a	49. c
5. a	20. b	35. b	50. b
6. c	21. a	36. a	51. c
7. d	22. c	37. b	52. a
8. c	23. a	38. c	53. b
9. b	24. b	39. c	54. b
10. c	25. b	40. d	55. d
11. d	26. c	41. b	56. a
12. c	27. d	42. c	57. d
13. b	28. a	43. a	58. c
14. c	29. b	44. c	59. c
15. a	30. c	45. b	60. b